HORSE *and* BUGGY DAYS

BY

KENT EUBANK

Illustrations by

BEN F. HAMMOND

WICHITA EAGLE CARTOONIST

KANSAS CITY, MISSOURI

BURTON PUBLISHING COMPANY

PUBLISHERS

Printed and Bound in the U. S. A

To The Wichita Eagle, Victor Murdock editor-in-chief and Marcellus M. Murdock, publisher, the best friends I ever had outside of my family—this book is dedicated.

CONTENTS

OLD-TIME MEMORIES REVIVED AT KENTUCKY PICNIC

Former Acquaintances Meet and Tell Tales of the Old Times Back in the Old Home State.

"Sing me a song of the sunny south, one with a sweet refrain;
Sing me a song of Dixie Land, that I may be happy again—
Sing me a sweet Southern melody, something of a bye-gone day—
Sing one song of my old Kentucky home, of my old Kentucky home far away."

The Kentuckians have come and gone. The picnic brought together many friends and former acquaintances, and it was a big success. We shook hands and said "how are you all getting along" just as we used to say it back in Kentucky, and talked about mint-julep, fox hunting, and the little log cabin back in the hills where we were born and I discovered that the log cabin home clings in the memory of every Kentucky son as if 'twere only yesterday. And I learned that to the others, like myself, in the darkest hours of life that little log house looms up as a guiding star, bringing to memory the lessons learned at mother's knee, and guiding us along a straighter and better road of life.

That little log house wasn't much to look upon, but the inside was always warm and bright, and the rafters rang with laughter and song when the children were gathered around the hearthstone for an hour of play.

Around that little house father plowed the ground and planted corn, and we children followed behind the plow and looked for fishing worms, then hied away to the creek to spend an afternoon angling among the drifted brush and logs in the streams.

In the evening after the chores were done, father planted cabbage plants and sweet potato slips, and set out tomatoes, and mother in her blue sun bonnet and gingham apron followed along with a pail of water and gave the plants the first life blood that started them on the way to the sun.

When the garden was planted father split palings in the woods and built a fence around the yard, trained the honey-suckle along the fence with bits of twine, and it grew apace and spread along the palings, and then bloomed and sent forth a fragrance that was sweeter than all the spices and myrrh of ancient lore. And father made a trellis in one corner of the yard, and a great crimson rambler grew toward the sky and seemed to glorify the whole place. He tinkered and tended here and there and in the summer the vegetables in the garden grew and mother went out before each meal to gather beans and corn and spuds and turnip greens, and the table was spread with such things, the like of which we seldom see again. And father bowed his head and said a prayer, and we children passed our plates "and fell to," and enjoyed every morsel that mother cooked.

Mother curtained the old log house with chintz, and put calico over the window panes, and she hung on the walls the pictures of "Pa" and her oldest son who had gone from home, and the pictures of my grandfathers and Uncle John, long since dead, but who had served in the legislature.

We boys cut the kindling, carried in the wood, slopped the pigs, and went to the spring and brought a pail of water for father to wash in when he came from the field. And sister washed the dishes, dried the skillets and rolled candle lighters, while mother skimmed the milk, and father stuck a board in the fire to save coal oil.

Then we children gathered around the big fire place and father read a chapter from the Bible and prayed that "saved we might be." And mother tucked us to bed, and the goodnight kiss is still warm on my forehead, regardless of the fact that time has brought a few streaks of gray among the once raven locks, and again I long for that dear old mother to

> "Tuck me to sleep in my old Kentucky home,
> Cover me with Dixie Skies and leave me there alone—
> Just let mother dear kiss my cheeks every morn—
> Let me lay there, stay there, never no more to roam."

Among old acquaintances I discovered Jim Curtis. Jim was a grown man with a dark flowing beard when I was a boy. He, with his little brood, lived in a log shanty on a rocky farm, and the soil in the hill district was not as good as it is in Kansas. Today Jim owns 320 acres of as fine land as can be found in western Kansas, and has just harvested a wheat crop that threshed an average of 20 bushels to the acre. He hasn't forgotten, however, that little log cabin back in Kentucky, and the whys and wherefores that caused him to leave. Jim wasn't connected with any feud which caused him to leave Kentucky and come to Kansas. He never stole any sang-digger hogs which caused him to leave the state. But if he tells me right he got disgusted with the country and his lot, and decided to "come west and grow up with the other green things," for the simple reason that one morning he got up from bed, washed his face, and was combing out his beard, when out hopped a lizard. Within a week he shaved off the beard and started to Kansas.

Old Jack Bedford is as good an old soul as ever left the Corn Cracker state, but like many another good man, he has his failings. Jack was raised back in the hills where the most the average citizen knew was moonshine whisky, and the most he ever did was "chew tobacco." Old Jack to this day loves his whisky and tobacco, and he uses them both. However, for the last few years old Jack has missed his whisky, and when he came to the picnic he came early and stayed late. He arrived Wednesday afternoon, and we met an old Kentucky moonshiner who now lives below the viaduct and dodges Chief Walston. This old Kentucky friend of ours had made a "little run" especially for the picnic, and old Jack "drank a quart of the new stuff and it flew to his head." We met him on the picnic ground and inquired "how are you getting along?" and he informed me that he came out early with a bad taste in his mouth and his insides burning up, until he fell in a vinegar barrel and found some of the best water.

I have got a boy named Jack, and he took in the picnic. I guess he saw it all and met most everybody that was there, at least when he came home at night he told me lots of things that I missed. Jack is eight years old, and he made his appearance in this world of bobbed hair and short dresses after we came West, but he has all the Kentucky traits of his mother. He told me about the foot races, the old-time fiddlers, the prettiest girl, the horse-shoe pitchers, and many other things too numerous to mention. Then I asked him: Jack, what was the funniest thing you saw? and he told me: "to see those old mammies shuffle when they tried to dance."

Jim Bledose is six feet two inches, and a born mountain climber. Jim was raised in the mountain section of Kentucky, and in his early years lost his appetite, but after coming to Kansas found one that belonged to a "hoss," and it stayed with him. I thought there was everything that any human being had partaken of back in old Kentucky, at that picnic, but Jim seemed, somehow, to be disappointed after meal time. At the tables he devoured two chickens, a small portion of a Kentucky ham, several hunks of cake, and enough bread and vegetables, I thought to feed a regiment, but still he had a hungry look on his face. Being one of the reception committee, whose duty it was to see that every Kentuckian had everything he wanted, I inquired of old Jim what the matter might be, and he told me he was hungry. There is no use being hungry here, I said, there is enough chicken and bread and hog and hominy left on the tables to feed a regiment come on and eat."

"Yes," he says, "there is plenty there, such as it is, and it's good enough what there is of it, but ever since I got here and got to talking about old times and the things we did and the things we had back in Kentucky, my mouth has been watering for cornbread and buttermilk and good old turnip greens."

I met old Jim Bevil on the picnic grounds and he seemed to be enjoying life at its fullest. Jim was a politician back in my home town when I was a boy, and for a number of years held the office of county court clerk. Politics was more bitter back there in the old days than they are in Kansas, and many were the tales told on the candidates—some true, some false, but they all had their place in the election. Jim was a Democrat, like everybody else back in that section of the country, but he had got out of line with the party leaders, and they scattered a report over the county that Jim had been mean to his wife, was about to desert her, and for several months had been sleeping at the home of one of his sons. A genuine Kentuckian has but little respect for a man who will mistreat or desert a good wife, and the report looked like it was going to tell in the final vote counting if old Jim couldn't square it. The thing that seemed to be losing him the most votes was the statement that he was sleeping at the home of one of his sons, so to correct this statement old Jim issued a circular, in which he said: "They say I don't sleep with my wife, and thus curtail my joys—well, this is strange, upon my life, friends, just look at my boys." And old Jim had ten, and he was elected.

Old Hamp Embertun, too, was at the picnic. Old Hamp has the largest machine shop in Kansas City, Kansas, and is rated as one of the wealthy citizens of the town, but I knew old Hamp back in Kentucky when he was as poor as a picked bird. Hamp run a blacksmith shop in Kentucky and had a big family. Back in the hill country money was not as plenty as the fleas on their dogs, and while Hamp shod horses and mended wagons and sharpened plows, his larder was not always overflowing. I was sitting on a rail fence talking with old Hamp one sunny afternoon, and like most men, when the wolf is howling close to the door, he was telling me his troubles. In the course of the conversation he told: "Here I am, old Hamp Embertun—can make anything out of iron any other 'ding man' can; can make anything out of wood any other 'ding man' can, and here I am, old Hamp Emberton, not worth a 'ding'." And he told me at the picnic that sitting on that rail fence I said to him, "Why don't you come to Louisville where you can make a living and get big wages for your work." And he told me, too, that the hungrier he got the more he thought of what I told him, and he come to Kansas.

Back in Kentucky when we had a picnic, or anything else that proved a success, we men folks all had to have a celebration, and I guess George Jones, Seth Hickerson, Dr. Chipps, Fred Cahal and J. J. Webb and myself were entitled to celebrate the night after the picnic. I don't remember whether these were the fellows or not—they are married men, but I am not hen-pecked—anyway, some of us fellows intended to celebrate like we used to back in old Kentucky, but that didn't make much difference. Our wives, as good wives generally do, got onto the racket, and when the picnic was over and I made an excuse to go down town that woman of mine got me by the back of the neck, and shook me like a bulldog shaking a fise. She weighs 180 pounds and I weigh 110, and my false teeth fell out of my pocket and I went home. And one or two of the other fellows' wives got them by the arm, and shook them, and said, "now, you walk it," and I noticed that they, too, walked it. And we didn't have no picnic celebration at all. Funny how us Kentucky fellows love and obey our wives, especially when they are bigger than we are.

This may all be a lie, and it may not, but howsomever, I believe every man at that picnic had a good time, and all went away saying:

> "I'd like to hear that song again. 'My Old Kentucky Home,'
> For I was born on 'Old Kentuck,' there's where I used to roam.
> I'd like to hear that song again, 'twould ease this homesick pain,
> Please, Miss, ask those Kentuckians to sing that song again."

THE OLD HITCH RACK

Where Men and Boys Congregated for Business, Pleasure and Gossip in the Horse and Buggy Days.

The challenging neigh of a horse or the anxious call of a brood mare to her colt is seldom heard along the streets of a city. Even in the smaller towns or at the county fair, one seldom hears the equine challenges and calls. But time was, when I was a boy, before the ascendency of the automobile, at a rally or a picnic or a fair or a camp meeting, in fact along any public street of any big or little city, village or hamlet, when the livelong day the neigh of horses and the whinny of colts strayed from their dams was almost as constantly ringing in one's ears as the barking of the man who sold peanuts or the one who dilated on the virtues of the tub of pink lemonade he was offering for sale at the circus. This was in the "good old days" of the hitch rack, the gathering place of the men folks on all occasions, and the place where most of the transactions of the countryside were carried out when the men met at some public gathering or in the town to while away the time and gossip with the brethren.

To the city man or the town man, for that, who was farm born or farm bred back in the old days, the neigh of a horse or the whinny of a colt on the streets would almost bring a feeling of homesickness. As I write in imagination I can hear the call of the dam and the answering whinny of a stocking leg colt—an answer that bore a note of terror and a note of joy, and methinks that an hour sitting on the fence of some barn yard listening to the cackle of hens, the grunting and squealing of swine, the lowing of cattle and the whinnying call of a mare to her colt over in the woods pasture would be an hour of unalloyed joy, but to sit on the chain of the old hitch rack, watch some "hoss and mule buyer" rub down the hocks of a three-year-old, discuss his limb qualities, look at his teeth punch his thumbs in his shoulder, evacuate a stream of tobacco juice, and say "turn him in the lot," would be about as near heaven as a man could get without going above.

The old hitching rack was the place of all places in the small towns and villages when I was a boy. It was here that all "hoss swaps" were made, all devilment planned, the new neighbor discussed, and the general gossip of the neighborhood spread.

The old hitch rack was the place where men and boys hitched their horses when they came to town. If it was in a county seat town the hitch rack was generally around the court house square. In all other towns it was along the main business street. Posts were set from 10 to 20 feet apart. The posts had a hole bored through the top, and through this hole a big chain was run clear along the line of hitch posts. To this chain the men and boys tied their horses by the bridle reins, and went about their business, happy and contented as a country yokel who has just parked a secondhand Ford in front of the town's general store and meandered over to the drug store to wave weak drinks with the town boys.

The greatest pride every fellow possessed when I was a boy was to hitch a high stepping bay to a top buggy, drive around the town square a few times and tie his horse to the hitch rack. If the buggy was new and shiny, and the horse a high stepper, reined high, every man and boy on the street would stop and look, and every damsel, and a few older women, would crane their necks to get a glimpse of the fellow with the pretty horse and new buggy. One particular fellow that I envied most in my younger days was Charlie Turner. Charlie was about my own age, and ran in my set. He drove the finest horses of any boy in the little town. On Sunday morning, just as the town folks were all coming from church, it was his practice to drive down the street, turn around the square a few times, then up to the hitch rack and tie his horse. The women stared and the maidens longed for a ride behind that beautiful bay, and he generally had his choice of the damsels for a Sunday afternoon's ride. It was vanity, pure and simple, but it won, and it eventually got him in trouble.

Other boys envied Charlie, and soon they began to guy him about his "crow bait." This continued for some time, then Charlie and Ned Turner met at the hitch rack, both driving beautiful bays. Envy overcame their better judgment, and a fight ensued. Charlie won in the fight, but got a term in the penitentiary. He served his sentence, and came back home. I used to see him sitting on the chain of the hitch rack, lonesome like, for his old associates didn't seem to take much stock in him after his return. Maybe the boys were right in passing him by, but I never thought so. To me the man who has paid and gone straight is a good step above the one who still owes and waits to make his peace with God until the day when he can hide nothing, and his puny, scheming little brain, that fooled men, is thrown open in the great book of time. But such was not the decree of the boys who met at the hitch rack.

Many funny things, too, happened at the old hitch rack. Men met there when they came to town, as a matter of course, and it became a habit to meet there to transact business, and while away the time. But when there was a horse or a mule or a cow to be sold at auction, the hitch rack was a place of business. John Steen, the town auctioneer, was selling a mule to the highest bidder. The bids were not going as high as Uncle John thought they should, and he was exhorting high, wide and handsome, when two men in the crowd started a fight. The crowd surged around as the fighters swayed across the street. By the time they were separated they were 50 yards from where Uncle John was standing in a spring wagon auctioning off the mule. The crowd began to scatter and it looked for a time as though he was going to lose his bidders. Finally, as a last resort, and in order to turn the crowd back in his direction, he roared until he could be heard for two or three blocks; "Now we'll start again on our most important business. There's nobody hurt except the man who failed to buy the mule."

Old John Gardner was the village sage. He could tell you more about your business in five minutes than you had learned in a life time, Old John, about twice a week rode up to the hitch rack on an iron gray mule that had seen better days. Judging from the looks and actions of that animal, it must have been a colt when old John was born, and old John's hair had passed the streak stage, and shone silver in the sunlight. John would ride up to the crowd sitting on the chain along the hitch rack, throw his right leg over the mule's neck, and sit for hours, telling the populace all about it. He also took a special delight in spreading all the gossip of the neighborhood, and never lost an opportunity to tell some of the misdeeds we boys had done. One day Old John was expostulating on the "Goneness of the Past," exposing some of the things the boys had done that should have been kept a secret, and it seemed that the longer he talked the less he told that was in strict accord with the —— commandment. Some of the boys, fearing Old John might stagger onto the truth, got an ounce of "high life," and when the old man was in the height of his glory, poured it along the back of the sleeping old mule. In a jiffy the mule's head went up, his ears pricked, his eyes popped out like they were on stems, and with a snort that could have been heard for four blocks, leaped into the air and went over the hill like a Bohunk dishwasher dodging the police. At the first jump of the old mule Old John lit in the street all sprawled out and considerably shaken up. When he got up, shook off the dust, in a tone as meek as a little lamb, Old John esplained: "I never saw that mule do that before," and all during the remainder of his life he would tell about his mule having a bad dream while standing at the hitch rack.

Buck Pedigo was a big mule buyer who lived at the railroad center, and each month came back in the hills to buy horses and mules. He was a good buyer, and the farmers with stocks to sell always met Buck at the hitch rack with their string. Buck had a son who had never been back in the hills, and on one occasion he brought him along. The boy was an overgrown yokel of 19 or 20 years, who had been raised as a parlor lizard. The day was hot, and he came out to the hitch rack carrying a parasol to protect his pink cheeks from the rays of the sun. Buck was buying a string of mules from Shanghi Cloyd, when they became involved in a dispute over the settlement. Cloyd called Pedigo a liar, and his young hopeful, anxious to take the part of his father, called out: "Knock him down pa!" Old man Cloyd turned an evil eye on the boy, looked him over for a few minutes, and with a frown that betokened more of sympathy than malice, told the young hopeful: "You come over and do it, you umbrella son-of-a-gun."

The horse swappers, too, from far and wide, met at the hitch rack to trade horses, and some good, and some bad deals were made. Jim Dunham was the prize horse swapper of the country, and Feland Turner had long looked for a chance to hook him. Dunham and Turner prided themselves on being the best traders in the world, and there was a strong feeling between them, each wanting to publicly get the better of the other in a trade. One day they met at the hitch rack and agreed to trade horses "sight unseen." Under the agreement each was to tell the other where to find the horse he had traded for. They were each to pick a man and send him after the horse, and the crowd could decide who had the better of the deal. Dunham's man went out to Turner's place and returned with four horse shoes he had taken off the dead horse. The crowd roared and gave Turner the "hoss laugh," while Dunham chuckled with delight at having put off a dead horse on Turner. Then Turner's man returned empty handed, to report that there was nothing to bring back, Turner had taken off the shoes when his horse died.

You could see many queer sights, too, if you watched the hitch rack, for most all things transpired there. But to me, I think the funniest thing I ever saw was a big John Indian and his family. John had come to town with his wife and six children in an old dilapidated road wagon. As he drove into town he spied a hearse coming from a funeral. This was the first hearse John had ever seen, and he thought it the prettiest wagon ever made, and so expressed himself. His squaw and all the little Indians also thought it a pretty wagon and wanted it, so John followed the undertaker home and struck up a bargain for the pretty wagon. The undertaker tried to explain to John the purpose of the hearse, and that he didn't want it, but to no avail. John wanted that wagon and so did all his family. In desperation the undertaker put the price so high he didn't think old John could buy it, but was surprised when the Indian went to the bank and soon came back with the money. Then old John hitched his little Indian ponies to the hearse, sat his wife and children down on the floor of the new wagon, shut the door, and all the rest of the afternoon he would drive around the square and return to tie up his ponies at different places along the hitch rack.

Allen Biggerstaff had bought a new surrey, and was proud of it. He drove into town and tied his team at the most conspicuous place along the hitch rack. A small crowd gathered at the new surrey and began discussing its peculiarities, its faults and its advantages. One of the boys said it was a phaeton, another said it was a surrey, several others gave names of various kinds, and finally Mr. Biggerstaff was called on to name his new outfit. And he explained by saying: "I don't know what you call it, but it's a dam good little wagon."

HOG-KILLING TIME

Blowing Bladders and Cooking Melts and Dog Fights and Kid Scraps Made Up a Day Long to Be Remembered.

When I tell you that there was more fun and satisfaction in living down on the farm 30 or 40 years ago, when I was a boy, some dude rancher of the present day is going to thank me for the buggy ride.

We fellows who grew up under the old dispensation can remember when going to bed at night we met ourselves getting up in the morning, when we had to do the work without any patent contraption to save muscle power, and a full dress suit consisted of a hickory shirt, a pair of blue jeans breeches, galluses our mothers knit after dad had sheared the sheep and our old negro mammy had carded the wool, and we remember, also, that there was no dissatisfaction or wrangling over the Farmers' Relief bill, no bootleggers and hijackers, and the stream of life flowed on like a pleasant dream.

It was the good old days before the girls began bobbing their hair, wearing light running togs and supporting their "sweeties," and the boys began devoting their leisure moments to painting their cheeks, marcelling their hair and depending on a short skirt for a package of cigarettes or a wad of chewing gum.

It was the good old days when our mothers wore linsey-woolsey and went barefooted during week days to save shoe leather, when sister's phonograph was a jews harp and father's automobile a spavined cayuse, and we were just as good and just as rich as our neighbor and our neighbor's children.

We had more holidays, more time to sit in the shade and reflect that it was good to be alive; more time to go fishing, not for men but for big mud cats and real suckers, and we didn't have to chase the dirty dollar like a hungry coyote camping on the trail of a corpulent jackrabbit to buy gasoline or a ticket to the movies. We were born at leisure, ate bread by the sweat of our brow, died from ripe old age, and we were acquainted, not only with our families, but with our neighbor's family, including the cat, dog and latest litter of pigs.

When we were boys our capital stock was our character—our reputation for honesty and uprightness—but today it's the dollar that is Almighty; it's the "cart wheel" that is the block and tackle which lifts the ill-bred bore into high society and puts the sap-head into the legislature, and sometimes I think we are raising a horde of cane-sucking dudes to daddy the next generation, instead of men of brain and brawn, character and respectability.

I saw a cake eater pass by my window, a cigarette in his mouth, a fire on one end and a fool on the other, and drifted off my original subject. All our boys are not like the bird who sidetracked me, for if a lot of them that are growing up today had him in a country where there was no law he would soon be praying for asbestos shoes and a drink of water.

What I started in to tell you about was hog-killing time as I remember it way back when I was a boy. The hog is the most disgusting animal the good Lord ever created, and though the process was pretty well started back in Biblical days, all the devils have never been cast out of the hog. Going on the Darwin theory the country is pretty well populated at this time with hogs, and a lot of them have only two feet. Yet if the farmer's smokehouse is fairly well stocked with this animal of the four-footed species when winter comes, he's mighty dog-gone well fixed to hibernate during cold weather, for I'm here to tell you that in a long and eventful career in which I have gulped down and digested everything from angel food to slumgullion, there is nothing in this life that gives better satisfaction than hog-jowl, corn-pone and good old turnip greens.

Hog-killing time is the greatest sport season of the year for the kids, and some of the old folks enjoy it. The season starts when the first blue winds whistle through the peach orchard and moan around the corner of the house. On this day father and the hired man set a big barrel antigodlin' in the ground, with just dip enough to scoot the hog in easy and pull him out without too much of an effort. We kids go out in the hills and gather in a wheel-barrow of limestone rocks and pile up hickory wood near the barrel. The barrel is then filled with water and the preliminaries are over. At 4 o'clock next morning mother calls us down to breakfast and then the fun starts. It is the job of us kids to keep the rocks hot, and we pile on the hickory wood. When the rocks begin to glow with a deep red they are dropped into the water barrel until the water is het to a proper scalding temperature. Ashes are poured into the water, it is claimed to make the hair slip, and then the hired man, or a neighbor who has joined us, knocks the hog in the head with an ax. Father, who is an expert at everything and admits it, sticks the hog, and we kids get into the play. Grabbing the 400-pounder by the hind legs we drag him to the scalding barrel and turn him over to father and the hired man. They ease Mr. Hog into the barrel, turn him over and over several times, drag him out, and all together, father, the hired man, we kids and the neighbor, fly into Mr. Hog like a duck on a June bug, and scrape the hair off in a jiffy. Next a gambrel stick is stuck into Mr. Hog's hind legs and he is strung up, and pa, who is still an expert, takes the sharpest, biggest butcher knife, rips Mr. Hog open, takes out his entrails, and the fight between the kids start. Long before Mr. Hog has been ripped open each kid has claimed the bladder, and father settles the matter by letting the "best man" have it. I never got the first bladder, but I got many a black eye fighting for it.

In the course of time we all get a bladder, and then the contest starts. Weeks beforehand we have slipped off to the swamp and cut a lot of reeds, dried 'em and are ready for the fray.

Did you ever blow up a hog bladder? If you never did you have missed the most fun in a boy's life. We blow, and blow, until that hog bladder grows as big as a baby balloon, in an effort to see which one of us can blow the biggest one without bursting it. And the boy who blows the biggest bladder is the champion to compete with the neighbor boys at the next hog-killing in the neighborhood. And a boy down on the farm, who is the champion bladder blower of the community is as much a champion as Wayne Munn in the wrestling game.

Then there is more fun from another angle, than blowing bladders. That's when you cook and eat the melt.

Say, boy! did you ever get a long stick, sharpen the little end, stick a hog melt on it, hold it over the fire and let it slowly sizzle away until it becomes brown and brittle? Of course you scorch your knuckles, singe your hair a bit, bake your cheeks, but when that melt is done, you go to take it off the stick and burn your fingers, drop it in the dirt, grab it up and brush it off, lick your chops and begin to eat—it is written that "you may sometimes see heaven without going above," and I always thought the fellow who wrote that must have had a well-cooked hog melt in his hand at the time.

Along toward the shank of the evening, the neighbors, always interested in what is going on, drop in to see how much net the big hog weighed, and along with them they bring their dogs. Just why a man would bring his dog to a hog-killing I never could figure out, but he does. Now, neighbors' dogs are not as friendly as neighbors' wives, and immediately trouble starts.

The old brindle cur dog, possibly on account of breeding, is mad at the world, and the smell of fresh meat adds to his already mean disposition, and he starts a fight with the hired man's Shepherd. Then when the fight starts all the neighbor kids take sides with one dog or the other, and while father, the hired man and all the neighbors throw buckets of water on the fighting dogs we kids shout with glee as first the cur and then the Shepherd gets a headlock or some other advantage in the fight. The argument among the kids waxes warm and by the time the dogs are separated the kids are fighting as hard as the dogs in the heat of their battle. Finally the kids and the dogs are separated, but many times are left with a dark brown taste in their mouths that lasts throughout the years, and causes strife and hatreds that last during the remainder of their natural lives, even going down to the graves with some of the brethren.

When the hogs are all butchered then the work begins. Of all things sad, all things dreaded and hated by the average boy, it is turning the sausage grinder. When I was a boy I longed for everything else but the time to come when dad sharpened his ax, for I had to turn the grindstone. It is a kid's job, but to this day I do not believe that an all-wise and merciful father ever intended for a boy to turn the sausage grinder, and there are plenty of old heads who will agree with me.

Grinding sausage 20 or 30 years ago was a slow job. The grinder was a small affair. The meat was cut in long strips and poked in the mouth of that grinder by mother while I turned, and turned and turned and prayed and cussed in the same breath, but it seemed that neither prayer nor cussing availed to a very great extent, for the more you turned and the more you ground the bigger the pile in the dish pan got, for dad, with a sharp butcher knife, and an appetite for sausage that he expected to last all winter, continued to cut those long strips and drop them in that dish pan, and dad could cut much faster than I could grind. If I had put the same amount of work into ditch digging as I put in turning that sausage grinder, I could have dug the Panama Canal, methinks, in a couple of winters.

But eventually the job, like most jobs of that kind, came to an end. Then mother cut up the sage and peppers, and worked it in like sour dough and biscuits, stuffed into a long poke, hung it up to the rafters in the smoke house, let it hang until some special occasion, like when the preacher came to our home for dinner, when all the good things were piled on the table at once, but when she took down a poke, cut it into rather thick slices and patted into round, flat cakes, fried it good and brown, nothing that has since been dished up on a French menu or by health experts was in the same class with the sausage that mother used to make.

There was just one thing that took the joy out of hog-killing time when I was a boy down on the farm, and that was the memory of pulling pursley to feed the brutes. No boy ever kicked on slopping the pigs, corning the hogs, or repairing the pen, but there has been many a good obedient boy left a happy home because dad made him pull pursely to feed the swine. Pursley is a weed of rank growth that flourishes in every well regulated garden. It puts no flesh on the hog, but the hog will eat it, just the same as it will eat everything else brought to the pen. Pursley ruins the garden patch, and every dad on the farm who makes a garden, and most of them do, thinks it a God-given duty, to make the boy pull that pursley and feed it to the hogs. And at hog-killing time, when we were blowing bladders or cooking melts, some old gray-beard who wanted to take the joy out of life, started an argument as to how much pursley that hog had been fed, and how good it was in mother and the girls to do the pulling while the boys went fishing, all of which was not true, for the boy had to pull the pursley, and it took a lot of joy out of life. Do you happen to remember when you pulled the cussed stuff? And didn't that have something to do with your leaving home and coming to town?

When some fellow asks me "how you going to keep 'em down on the farm?" I tell him, have more hog-killing times and less pursley pullings, and the soda fountains won't harbor so many cowboys.

HOW TIMES HAVE CHANGED SINCE WE WERE YOUNG!

Father Cut Wheat with a Cradle and Rode Behind a Yoke of Steers, but His Son Uses a Combine and an Automobile.

How times have changed since we were young!

With the women voting and the girls cavorting and the boys flivvering and the men golfing, some folks claim that the country is hairstrung and windshook over the bottomless pits of perdition, but I don't know.

Twenty years ago I rode from Wichita to Kingman behind a pair of high-stepping bays, hooked to a light buggy, and it took me the greater part of a hot day to make the trip.

Forty years ago I made a trip from Tompkinsville to Glasgow, Kentucky, a similar distance, behind a yoke of oxen hitched to a tar-wheel wagon and it took the greater part of four days.

Last week I went from Wichita to Kingman with "Oley Olsson" in a Studebaker and we made the round trip in less than three hours, scouted a couple of oil wells and ate dinner in a Wichita chili joint.

As we drove back from Kingman I counted 27 combines cutting and threshing wheat in the fields between Kingman and Wichita, and I thought oh! what a change since we were young.

Out on the Kingman road lives old John Bledsoe and his wife, Mary. John Bledsoe is not his right cognomen, but he lives there just the same. I use an assumed name for the reason that John got in trouble back in Kentucky, some 20 or 30 years ago, and is not overly anxious to have the neighbors know his past history.

The trouble started at the county fair, when Bill Ray's hog carried off the blue ribbon, and when the smoke cleared away and the coroner performed his duty, John though it best to come to Kansas where the country was new, for back in Kentucky, 30 years ago it was a sad thing in many ways to get tangled up in a hog fight at the county fair, especially if both men had relatives, and they generally had.

John's hog was in close competition for the blue ribbon. It stood two feet seven inches high. Bill's hog was not quite so tall by an inch or two, but measured a few inches longer from the snout to the tip of its tail.

I stopped at John's house on the way back from Kingman, and in talking over old times asked him: "How much did the prize hog weigh?" and he told me 59 pounds.

Then he showed me over his hog lot on his Kingman farm, and his prize hog weighed 487 pounds, but he insisted that Bill's hog was a better hog in that section of Kentucky at that time, than his pure-bred Poland China today, for the reason that back in Kentucky at that time the best hog was the one that could run the fastest when an acorn fell from the top of a 100-foot tree.

As Bill Ray passed out of the hog prize competitions back in Kentucky at that time, so he passes out of this story, but old John Bledsoe plays an important part.

John had 240 acres of wheat, and his boy was cutting and threshing that wheat at the same time, riding under the shade of a silk umbrella smoking a cigarette and wearing balloon unionalls, on a cushioned seat of a combine pulled by a tractor, and was cussing because a farmer had to work so hard during harvest time.

I asked Aunt Mary, that's old John's wife, if she ever saw old John cutting wheat when he was a boy, and she told me:

"Lord sakes, child! yes; but I never saw him cut any wheat that away, for things have changed mightily since we were young. That's how I happened to fall in love with John. That was before the days when farming had become a profession and the tillers of the soil had none of the conveniences of today. Those were the days when men were famous according to their ability to 'cut off the heels of a rival cradler'—for John cut wheat then with a cradle —and they were the days when manhood was counted by strength—strength in every form rather than by cunning.

"John had gone to the wheat field early in the morning and was cradling the wheat with might and main. An hour or so later I came swinging down the road with a milk pail in my hand and wearing a blue gingham bonnet. I peeped through the worm fence to see how the wheat was ripening, and a faint sound reached my ear. It was John cutting the wheat with a cradle, the only means they had in those days.

"As I watched him I thought, my what a sweep! as he swayed to and fro in all the rhythmic grace of the cradler's stride, swinging easily now backward, the curving blade, and then forward into a cutting sweep, clean and swift, laying the even swath. On John came, cradling in mighty sweeps, cutting the swath clean out to the end where I stood by the fence. He hung his cradle on a thorn tree and came and sat on the fence, and a few days after harvest John and me were married, and have been ever since, but

I have never seen him cutting wheat bestride a tractor, under an umbrella and wearing store clothes at the time. He cut it with a cradle, and I helped him thresh it with a flail, and we didn't think it very hard work either."

John and Mary came to Kansas when the country was sparsely settled, but they have done their share in increasing the population. Along with raising wheat and hogs they have raised three boys and two girls, and a barn lot full of chickens and a few calves, and are now prosperous and happy.

As Aunt Mary was telling me about John's wheat-cutting days her oldest daughter, with bobbed hair and painted lips, drove up in a big automobile, and I asked the good old lady of yesteryear her opinion on the automobile, and she told me:

"I don't know much about the automobile and the petting parties, but I used to be wise on a horse and buggy. When I was a girl the horse and buggy ride gave us as big a thrill as the flivver gives the boys and girls today, and I think a great deal more. It was the rule in the horse and buggy days for us girls to hold the lines while our best beaus held our hands. I hear that some of the boys and girls try to keep up with us old folks in our younger days by trying this rule on the flivver, but it don't work. When they try it now more often than not they take their best girl along with them to the hospital and dad's flivver to the junk yard."

And then I told Aunt Mary: "The petting parties in the automobile may be all right, but to my mind it in no way compares with an old-time chat in the parlor. The automobile some times runs out of gas, or gets a punctured tire, and then there's always some fool motor-cycle cop coming along to interfere and order you to move on. But then we had similar troubles in the parlor: There was the old man who retired early, and he seemed to take a delight along about ten o'clock in yelling 'bed time.' That's another way in which the times have changed since we were young."

How well do I remember the fun I have had in one of those old-time parlors, and the song we boys used to sing: "Behind the parlor door! behind the parlor door! the old man he got tired and stamped around the floor, while I was having lots of fun behind the parlor door."

There is another thing, too, Aunt Mary told me, that has changed since we were young. "The girls then helped their mothers in the kitchen and learned the art of cooking and sweeping the dirt under the stove or the dresser instead of building nut sundaes and drawing a salary with which to buy powder and paint for their lips. If the boys of today played the same old games of snap up that we used to play, and kissed their girl every time he caught her, I am afraid that most of the boys of today would die of painter's colic."

Yes, times have changed, I told Aunt Mary, in many respects since we were young, but in nothing possibly aside from cutting wheat and raising hogs as much as in our women.

I have no objection to the new woman, but for the life of me I can't figure her out as an equal to her grandmother. Raised on malted milk, chocolates and ice cream, all the drug stores in the country can't put the roses in her cheeks that her grandmama had. The drug store complexion may be all right, but to us old timers it don't shine like unto the days of old.

Reared beneath the some times sunny skies of the great outdoors, grandmama did not need any drug store to catch and hold her "sweetie." Born of poor but honest parents she grew up guarded from every pitfall, an impulsive child of nature. A liberal diet of sow belly and corn pone, encouraged in its onward march by liberal gourds of buttermilk and an occasional dessert of sorghum molasses, rapidly rounded out her lissom form, and running barefoot over the pastures after the cows, or down to the milk gap—and say, the prettiest sight the good Lord ever created is a blue gingham bonnet with red ribbons on it, bobbing up and down beside a thin flanked cow about sunset at the milk gap—gave her the majestic carriage which Juno might have envied.

But oh! what a contrast, I told Aunt Mary, is the average girl of today. I saw a fair sample just a little while ago coming out of the drug store. She was a beautiful little eye tonic, and appeared overly anxious to locate a meal ticket until parted by the divorce courts. Judged by all standards she was an exquisite picture. Her eyes were lustrous, limpid and full of soft splendor; her hair bobbed and curled after the fashion, was a veritable crown of glory. The color of her skin was undescribably beautiful, soft tinted, contrasting with the coral of her mouth so exquisitely moulded. She walked along close to the big brick building. As she passed beneath an open window a bucket on the sill tipped over and the liquid showered upon her. In the building they manufactured paint remover. And oh what a change.

As old John Bledsoe started out to the wheat field to see how the son in his youthful strength was getting along cradling wheat under a silk umbrella on a cushioned seat of a combine, I started for the Studebaker to come to town, I heard Aunt Mary say:

"Yes, times have changed since we were young."

FIRST SETTLERS IN "NO MAN'S LAND"

Lon Wilson Wins First Battle With the Cowboys Without Bloodshed and Without a Cross Word.

Only a few short years ago the problem of converting the prairies of western Oklahoma, then a cattle country, into a land flowing with milk and honey, with wheat fields waving in the summer sun, occupied the minds of men who spend their lives in the study of social questions, and each year the study reverted to the prairie lands of western Oklahoma.

The fundamental idea was that no land, no matter what the manner or the profit of its use, has come to its best until the home, the little white schoolhouse and the church have taken root in it—until the family ties bind home and country together, and the home builders have put their sweat and blood into it—have laid to rest a mother, a father or a child under the weeping willow which shadows the little church yard—have established themselves in it and become a part of it—not as adventurers but as home builders.

In the western section of Oklahoma, in that beautiful prairie section once known as "No Man's Land," which even to the present time is partly given over to stock raising, is one of the most fertile sections of country to be found in the Sooner state. For many years there was no permanent settlement in this strip of Oklahoma, and the big ranges have only been broken up within the past 15 or 20 years. For a long time it was the struggle between the small farmer and the stock men for the possession of the land and the war that was waged was fierce and bitter.

It was in this section of country that Joe Black was punching cattle for the Coronado Cattle Company when old John Wilson moved to the valley and staked a claim on 640 acres of government land Uncle Sam had set aside for the homesteader.

From the day Joe Black entered the employ of the big cattle company all the energy he possessed was given to the mastery of the life and the work. He set himself to know the cattle business thoroughly. Soon after his arrival the company bought out, consolidated and reorganized a number of smaller ranches, and Joe was given the foremanship of one of the camps.

Less than a year after his first employment he was made supervisor and given general oversight over the dozens of herds scattered over the Coronado range. Then by a sort of inevitableness he gained the title and place as manager of the company holdings.

Although much was demanded of him by his superiors he was trusted implicitly, not only for the proven integrity of his accountings, but because of his shrewd ability.

It had been his one ambition since coming to the range to climb above the little ranch foremanship or manager, to be one of the partners in the big game, and some day he hoped to speak with authority, not only in the interest of others, but for himself as well. At any rate he meant to be rich, strong and powerful; but at the present time the future was looking pretty blue.

Spring is about the only season in which the gods send much rain in the cattle country, and every drop counts in the toil of the year's wellbeing. If the rains fail the grass is scant; even the fresh shoots of sage brush are short and bitter; and without good pasture the herds come into the winter months gaunt and weak, ready for a heavy toll of death during the winter months.

Joe had come 40 miles in the saddle since morning, beneath brassy skies, his narrow eyes noting the wan hue of the range land, and because of this situation his mind was troubled.

The foreman of the camp had come in, unsaddled his pony, and stood by the fire, waiting for the questions Joe always asked when on his rounds of the camps.

He was a lean, active old man, this Walt, upon whose scant bearded face the years rested lightly. He chewed his tobacco with a short, quick jerk of the jaws when a little uneasy, and he was uneasy now, for he had no good news to tell Joe on this trip.

"How's the water below?" Joe asked after a moment. Walt turned his tobacco to the other side of his mouth, spit in the coals, and shifted from one foot to the other.

"Fair," he answered. "The creek is drying up in spots, but the holes are mostly fair." Then, after a few minutes silence, he added:

"A couple of settlers filed on the Blue Ride springs last week, taking 640 acres each, which covers all the water for the west range, and will cut out a lot of good pasture, unless you get rid of them."

Joe's scowl deepened, but he brooded the news in silence. "Settlers." The word meant much to Joe Black and his future plans on the range. In the dry season water from these springs determined the use of thousands of acres of the Coronado's free range in this section of their psature.

South of the springs another outfit had been running cattle for years, but always staying on their own territory by a tacit agreement upon an imaginary line. In the last year or so, Joe had learned, these herds had outgrown the range, and it occurred to him that the settlers were men from the other ranch hired to jump the springs, not as bonafide settlers but to hold the water for them.

"And they have not only filed on the claims, but are living there, one of them has a family—and a deuce of a pretty girl," Walt ventured after a short pause, "and they are plowing and fencing their claims at the same time."

Joe got up, walked out into the night and brooded over the situation. The stars shone feebly through a summer dust haze, and he saw no sign of rain. He had hoped for a good year, for it had been generally understood that at the end of the season, with the right kind of a showing, this year would make him a partner in the Coronado Company, and that had been his one ambition since coming to the range. For this reason the settlers worried him more than his looks betrayed.

Early next morning he started for the next camp, some 30 miles away, but turned aside from the trail to ride down by Blue Ridge springs and investigate. The more he thought about the settlers the more it worried him, and he was anxious to know the character and kind of men he had to deal with.

When he arrived at the springs what he saw was far from what he had expected and not at all to his liking. The springs were necessary to that part of the company's grazing lands, and in dry weather, when all other water supplies failed, the pools near the springs were always full, although the stream sunk in the sand about a mile from the source. Besides, the grove around the springs had for many years been an ideal camping place for the cowboys and generally referred to as their haven of rest.

The homesteader's camp was pitched at the edge of the grove. Near the camp was a pile of lumber and logs, the beginning of house and barn and corral building. Above the springs a line of new fence posts lay along the ground ready for setting. The two claims of 640 acres each covered all the water from the springs until it sank into the sand, and the fence would shut the water in completely, even in times when the stream carried its full volume. One of the men was plowing across the flat, and Joe rode over to form the acquaintance of his new enemies. The man stopped his horse at Joe's approach and stood waiting.

"Hello!" he laughed, with friendliness. "Hello!" Joe responded. "Where do you come from?" he asked briefly.

"Kentucky," the young man answered. "Dad thought land was too high there, so we decided to try a different locality. This is sure different, but I guess we'll like it. Dad's going to run cattle on the range here. It looks like mighty poor grass to me, but they say it keeps them alive all right, if you've got water. We are starting with 50 cows till we see how they do, and how much feed we can raise."

Joe realized at once that they were settlers who had come to stay. This meant that if they "stuck" next year others would follow, and it would be only a short time until all the range would be taken up. But he reckoned that if the worst should develop it would be easier to deal with private claimants than with a rival company.

The sound of a horn broke the stillness, and the young man began unhitching the horses from the plow. "That's dinner," he said. "Come on and get a bite. It's a little lonesome here with no neighbors closer than 20 miles." Joe was both hungry and tired, and he wanted to see more of the settlers with whom he had to deal, so he followed the young settler to the corral and on to the shack of a house.

The Wilson family consisted of old John Wilson, his wife, son Ned, and daughter, Gertrude, the queen of the household.

As Joe followed the young man from the corral to the little shanty he saw old age and youth standing together on the threshold. With poetic fitness the past was typified by an elderly gentleman, white haired, keen eyed, and lightly touched by the weight of years; while by his side stood a slender and beautiful girl whose easy carriage and well developed, though dainty figure, were eloquent of perfect health. She was a tall, handsome young woman, remarkable not only for the wealth of ruset-brown hair that crowned her shapely head, but for a complexion and grace of that rare blend of truly southern type. As Joe gazed upon the young woman his heart was somewhat softened toward the settlers whom he had decided he and his cowboys would soon run out of the country.

It was a month before Joe made the rounds of the different cattle camps and got back to the homesteaders. The weeks had been particularly busy ones for him, so he had given but little thought to the settlers until he found himself nearing the Blue Springs camp.

After rounding up his work at this camp it occurred to him that he had better pay a visit to Blue Springs and see how the settlers were progressing, and the early morning sun shone down on a handsome young cowboy with-shining spurs and polished boots, riding straight to the settler's cabin, and every month thereafter when Joe come to the camp he always rode over to see how the settlers were getting along—and to see Gertrude.

A year rolled by and Joe and his cowboys had not attempted to run the settlers out of the country, but he paid regular visits to their home, and many an evening he and Gertrude strolled out in the moonlight and told life's sweetest story in the most endearing terms.

It was late in the autumn and Joe had just returned from the East with a large shipment of cattle. On this trip he had been taken into the company as a partner. After supper he and Gertrude walked out to the springs where they could be alone. The sun was just going down over the top of a distant hill and the man and woman stood side by side, and the golden light seemed to envelop them like a tender benediction. Around them and about them was no other living soul—they were separated from the world of men and women. As they gazed at the entrancing vista a wandering bird alighted on a bough of a great cottonwood close beside them, cheeping a little noisily. Gertrude listened with pleasure in her soft brown eyes, a smile on her parted lips, and the hand which was imprisoned in her lover's trembled a little with sheer pleasure—and the settlers then and there won in their battle against the cowboys.

LOVE FOLLOWS TO OKLAHOMA PLAINS

Only to Find Another Love, Which Though Tortured by the Country's Whim, Is Made Perfect in the End.

It is written that love can save a bad man as easily as it can wreck a good one according to the mysteries of human nature, as be like the peace of God himself, past all understanding.

When Nellie Harbison left her Kentucky home with her parents to settle in Oklahoma and prove up a homestead, she left behind an ardent lover in the person of Ed Davis, her playmate and sweetheart since childhood.

As they stood on the platform at the depot Ed told Nellie for the first time that he loved her, and in a year would come to Oklahoma and ask her to become his wife.

Oklahoma was yet a cattle country at that time, and Will Moody owned a large ranch adjoining the claim on which old man Harbison filed for a homestead. Moody was an almost irresistible lover as well as a worker. His handsome face, his wild, reckless manner and his dashing wooing were altogether unlike the diffident, unobtrusive manner of Ed Davis.

Ed Davis had loved Nellie for a long time, but never told her so; it was not his nature. Will Moody loved Nellie too, and told her so over and over again. He laid his heart, his love, his life at her feet, sang cowboy love songs with her as his heroine; talked always of her beauty and grace and perfection until every one in the surrounding country knew he was in dead earnest in his courtship.

When Ed Davis came to Oklahoma and asked Nellie for her answer, she simply said "I am very sorry, Ed I have always thought a great deal of you, but I love Will Moody."

"Then you can never be mine," he said simply. "I wish you all the happiness that his love can give, and if the time should ever come when you need a friend, think of me; I would go to the farthest end of the earth to serve you."

A month later when the ground was clothed in white, and the Christmas season was drawing near, Will Moody led Nellie Harbison to the marriage altar and they were made man and wife.

Ed Davis said nothing of his sorrow. Few knew the secret of his love and his rejection. He located in Alva and entered the practice of the law. Fortune favored him as it always does the brave, and in a few years he had attained ease and competency.

As Nellie and Will stood before the altar—he so handsome and manly, she so fair and sweet, the homesteaders said that the sun had never shone upon a more beautiful sight than their wedding, and to Nellie Harbison the bright summer months that followed her marriage were one long golden dream.

In this life, so full of care and pain, it is something to be thankful for to be entirely and perfectly happy for only a short time, but both Nellie's and Will's happiness was made complete when the second year after their marriage a son was born.

The years rolled on and the little fellow grew apace. He was the idol, not only of Nellie and Will, but of the whole ranch, and the cowboys that rode the trails on adjoining ranches. He was of a rambling disposition and had been found several miles from home at various times. He had a large Collie dog to which the little fellow was much attached, and the dog always accompanied him on his ramblings.

One December day the little boy and the dog were missing. All the afternoon the distracted mother sought her boy, but in vain, and one after another of the cowboys who returned to camp had not seen him. Then every one turned out and all night the lonely canyons echoed to the broncho's tread. Morning came, but no tidings of the lost boy. On the second day as one of the cowboys was riding through the tall grass at the head of a canyon he was attracted by the feeble bark of a dog, and on nearing the spot found the little boy, and with a sorrowing heart and tearful eye he hurried back to the ranch to lay the lifeless body in the mother's arms.

It is said that troubles never come singly. The death of their little son, their pride and joy, had cast a shadow over the lives of Nellie and Will, and there was an empty void in the home.

In the spring the young grass began to shoot up early and it looked like a prosperous year for the range, but the rains failed to come and the grass was late in getting a start. By early summer the hot winds had parched the grass into a crisp. The cattle had to be shifted from pasture to pasture, and even in the middle of summer they were much weakened, and when winter came they were in poor condition to face the cold and wind and the death toll was heavy and the loss exceedingly great. When the time came to ship from the ranch there was a heavy slump in the market, and the loss told materially on the financial circumstances of Will Moody.

Then it was that Nellie, the broken-hearted mother, began to perceive spots on the sun. They sold the ranch and moved to town, and Will, still stout hearted, went to work at the stock yards. But with the death of his little boy and his loss in the cattle business Will's pride was crushed, and he began to drown his sorrows in the flowing bowl and at the gambling table. His passion for drink and gambling grew with each succeeding week. As long after pay day as his money held out he would play in the biggest games and buy drinks freely for the crowds. Two years had passed since Will and Nellie left the ranch and moved to town, and drink and gambling had made him only a wreck of his former self.

One evening Will was late, as usual. As he entered the room Nellie gazed in speechless alarm at his ghastly face. He took her hand in his. His white lips moved, but he could not speak. Never had she gazed upon a face so full of wild despair as his. She knelt by him and clasped her slender arms around him. She soothed his tears as a good and gentle woman alone can soothe in despair. Little by little she drew from him the story of his distress. As he started home he stopped in the saloon. He began to gamble and lost. When the last of his money was gone he went back to the safe at the little office and took out a packet of bills—five hundred dollars in all. He continued to gamble and lost—lost to the last sou. The money belonged to the firm and when business opened next morning his theft would be discovered.

Nellie's face grew as white as his own. The money must be replaced, but how? There was no place in the world where Will Moody could borrow that amount of money. Then she thought of Ed Davis living in Alva, 20 miles away. She remembered what he had said when she rejected him for Will Moody, "If you ever need a friend come to me." And she went to Ed Davis in her trouble.

Will Moody was the first one at the office next morning. He placed the money back in the safe, and his crime was sealed in the breast of himself, his loving wife and his God.

He never seemed to realize the heart-ache, the humiliation and the shame his freedom had cost her. He played a stiff, close hand, but had been spared, and he counted it luck. His passion for drink and gambling seemed to grow and Nellie was more and more neglected, until her patience exhausted, she attempted to take Will to task about it, when he lost his temper and rained heaping abuse upon the head of his little wife.

Then the world became blurred to her; she was running wildly down the lane toward the heart of the village, direct to her father's home, and in the arms of her mother, told her she had left Will Moody and would never live with him again.

When a man has allowed his animal nature to overcome his moral sense he is in a pretty bad plight. This had been Will's trouble, and he realized it only when it was too late.

Will spent the next year hanging around the town, working at odd jobs and spending what little wages he earned in the saloon or squandering it over the gambling table, but was always thinking that Nellie would come back to him. But as time went by and she did not return, and his every attempt to see her was refused, he began to realize that all was lost, and to long for the old cow days on the plains. The vision of his little boy would haunt him, and at midnight's holy hour he would wander out to the little graveyard and sit in solitary meditation. His old time friends had shaken him now, and he realized that if he could not find new life in the cow country the game was not worth the price.

Saddling his pony one morning he started for the north where the herds roam at will over the wild prairies, and the past is hidden in the days that are gone.

He rode into a cattle camp owned by Ed Davis late one evening. It was the branding season and Ed was taking a vacation at the ranch. He saw Will coming and recognized him at a distance. He told his foreman to put Will to work at top wages, give him every advantage but not to let him know who was the owner of the ranch. And Ed Davis drove back to town before Will saw him.

Taken away from the city and his old haunts, with no saloons and no temptations he soon forgot his appetite for whisky and gambling and began to regain his old manhood. During the season he worked in the branding pens and the foreman observed that he was not only an expert cowboy, but took an interest in the affairs of the ranch, and when the branding season was over Will found himself in possession of a steady job. Ed Davis had seen to this when Will first came to the ranch. There was nothing on the range for which he could spend his money, no friends to invite him to take a drink, and the end of each month found his salary tucked away in his pockets, and deep down in his heart the old yearning for Nellie. His one ambition was to make good, go back to the woman he loved, again win her love and respect, and in the days to come atone for the past.

Then old man Chism, the ranch foreman, fell ill with the flu. His age and his life in the open were against him, and he lingered only a few days and died. He had no known relatives, and his last will and testament gave to Will Moody his one-half interest in the ranch, which Ed Davis had given him for this particular purpose, after he became ill.

And Nellie never forgot Will Moody. He had forced her to leave him, and in his drunken rage had struck her—but she loved him still although she had made up her mind never to see him again.

Since her little boy died it had been the rule of Nellie's life to visit his grave every Sunday night, and sit for an hour in the gloom thinking of the happiness she had enjoyed in the days when Will sat by the hearthstone, a loving and faithful husband, and she pressed her babe to her breast and sang him to sleep.

All that autumn the sweet face of Nellie had haunted Will Moody, and in his visions he would see the little mound that covered their boy. The vision haunted him more and more, as the weeks and months rolled by. Then one day business connected with the ranch called him back to town. All day he rode through the blazing sun, and as the shades of night began to fall he could see the lights of the town. As he drew nearer the thoughts of his dead boy kept haunting his mind. As he rode alongside of the cemetery he dismounted, dropped the reins to the ground, and with head bent low groped his way through the shadows to the sacred spot.

It was Sunday evening and Nellie was kneeling beside the little grave, but was concealed behind a clump of rose bushes she and Will had planted shortly after their little boy was laid in the cold and silent tomb.

Will walked straight to the little grave, took off his hat and laid it on the ground, then knelt on the opposite side from Nellie. "As he knelt by the little mound the moon shot out through a rack of clouds, and each recognized the other. There they knelt, one on each side of the little grave and looked coldly upon each other. Then they looked down upon the little mound that held the broken link with which God had bound their hearts. As they knelt they bowed their faces upon the cold sod that covered the dust of their sacred dead. They stretched forth their hands across the little grave, each to the other, and the Angel of God washed all the bitterness of the years from their hearts with a rain of penitential tears, and sent them down life's pathway hand in hand as in the old days when love was lord in their lives and the lost babe was cradled upon its mother's breast."

MY OLD KENTUCKY HOME

Men and Women from the Blue Grass and the Pennerile to Meet in Wichita September 1 in Their Second Big Picnic.

"I'd like to hear that song again,
My Old Kentucky Home,
For I was born in Old Kaintuck,
There's where I used to roam—
I'd like to hear that song again,
For it would ease my pain,
Please, Miss, go ask the singer
To sing that song again."

The Kansas Kentuckians have announced another picnic for September 1, and it takes me back to childhood days, before I came away.

Looking back over the years to my boyhood days I see a summer evening in my old Kentucky home. Faint radiance from a not long departed sun tints skies already dusky with the coming night. Beneath, the far shimmering expanse of the Cumberland river, its placid surface faintly ruffled at the capricious touch of truant airs, are reflected the fading glories overhead. From the western bank heavy foliage, in intermittent clusters, lengthens its shadows across the water. Here and there breaks in the leafy barrier's permit, on either shore, shelving margins of sand, and beyond, gently sloping bottom corn fields stretch away to dimly outlined hills, their wooded contours vague and misty. Save the dwindling radiance, no light braves the gathering darkness. Whispering eddies, drowsy bird notes, the splashing fin of some denizen of the waters; over all the inscrutible hush of night.

Across the mirroring bosom of the stream two shadows drift, wraithlike, yet urging onward. Tiring paddles ripple the water. Responsive to the wearied yet sturdy arms, they merge into the gloom of the western bank. Their frail bottoms grate upon the sloping sand, as the toilers in the fields return from their day's labors.

Over the leaf crowned eastern hills, the moon, threading the opening measures of its nightly march, floods valley and stream with a dim radiance as the men disembark and come up the road to consume a frugal meal and seek in slumber respite from the labors of the day.

The scene vanishes and across the vision of memory comes another season. It is the Christmas season—drifted snow; brown leaves on the oaks, rustling in the wind; a leaden sky with a smear of white from the house chimney like a scar across it; the odor of burning wood. Inside the house the smell of savory fowls browning in the oven; heaps of apples and walnuts and hickory nuts; golden brown pies and pastries and sweet potatoes baking in the "dog oven" over the coals on a cheerful hearthstone.

Blood-red berries shine resplendently amid the dark green foliage of moss wreaths, while bits of mint, sacred plant of the ancient Colonels, at unexpected places lend their aid to bashful swains or impudent merry makers.

The air is filled with the prattle of childish voices, joyous beyond comprehension over the latest gifts the good St. Nick has left them. Above the shrill trebles the tones of older voices none the less vibrant with happiness for their share in Christianity's greatest festival—Christmas Day.

It is the season of joy in the Old Kentucky home, of gladness and peace on earth, good will toward men. It is the day wherein no slightest thought of sorrow is allowed to mar the happiness of any member of the family. But all too true as I grew to older years it seemed to me, just such a thought intrudes upon the mind of patient loving mother. Tired with the endless round of duties that were necessary to the success of the day, but never for a moment did she forget the happiness of her children, for no Kentucky mother ever spared herself for the happiness of her child. And looking back through the mists of the years there comes a vision of the mothers of the hill country. These are the mothers who wore the sunbonnets; they worked in the field in the day time to help get food for the family in winter, and did their housework at night. When this was done they reached up to the shelf, took down the family Bible, read a chapter, and the family knelt in prayer.

Kentucky has lost one of the attributes upon which part of its charm formerly was based—good old "likker"—but she still retains, however, her fast horses, beautiful women and loyal sons.

The "old master" who took his whisky straight three times a day, intermingled with sprays of mint picked along the spring branch, is also passing, but his memory, too, lingers with us older boys. The broad brimmed hat and the gray goatee is more plentiful among the professional Kentuckians in various big cities than they are today in the land of the "kunnels;" the soft drawl is becoming a more snappy affair, and even the great colonial homesteads with far flung porches and spacious grounds are giving way to the smaller homes, and the wear and tear of the family automobile is destroying the need for a stately avenue of trees leading up to the old-time mansion in the Blue Grass section of the state. But the memory of the old-time Kentucky "kunnel," his servant and his frequent "nips" are memories that will never pass out of the minds of the older boys.

The quality of the old-time "kunnel's likker" was his pride and his joy, and the old servants would play on his vanity by bragging on the quality of his cellar. At one time we visited the home of an old-time "kunnel," and heard this conversation between the master and his colored attendant:

"Mr. Beck, dis toddy sho' tastes good. 'Taint scorchy like dat white stuff which dey stews up in de city, biles it in a coal-oil can wid concentrated lye. Folks drink dat pisen and it makes dem climb trees backwards.

"Mr. Beck, you knows old Sim? White feller? Got a shanty boat down at de far end of dis lake? He's ninety-three years old, and nigh dead. His woman had him lyin' on a bunk wid a mustard plaster to his stummick an, a bottle o' hot water to his feet. Sim was gone, couldn't lift a finger, couldn't wiggle narry toe. Well, suh, dat woman poured him just one drink 'o white lightnin', and dat stuff sho' did put de pep in Sim. Sim blinked a time or two, den riz up on his elbow an' say, 'Mandy, reach in dat glass o' water and gimme my false teeth—I'm jist bound to bite you."

It was only a few years ago that Kentucky ranked fourth in the Union in illiteracy. Today illiteracy is rapidly approaching the zero point. In 1912 Cora Wilson Stewart, county superintendent of Rowan county, decided to make an effort to eradicate illiteracy from the state. She announced that the schools of her county would conduct "moonlight" sessions, the schools to be open to all comers.

Whether Rowan county was a "moonshine" district or not, the idea appealed to the people. They came. And they kept on coming, whether the moon shone or not. On the first night of their opening 1,200 grown-ups attended, thirsty for knowledge. It was found that night schools were just as practical in the country districts as in cities. Attendance was probably romantic. The people were neighbors. Coming together on the common basis of ignorance, they found that they could have a delightful time getting knowledge.

The night schools have brought the moonshine of knowledge to thousands of people in the mountain regions of Kentucky, and illiteracy in the state has rapidly disappeared. It is said it was found necessary in some districts when the schools were first established, and at certain times, to hang up an artificial moon for the opening of the session of a school, but once opened it remained opened, and plenty of teachers were found for the work.

The old Hatfield-McCoy fued, the bloodiest war that ever infested a single community, was wiped away by the moonlight schools. The trail of death which lasted for 20 years started over the ownership of a "sang-digger" hog, and before the reign of blood ended 120 lives had been wiped out by the rifle and the six-shooter. But old Mother Hatfield and old Mother McCoy started attending the moonlight schools. They saw the light that led to a higher knowledge and a higher being, and they laid the foundation which wiped out the bloodiest murder period in the history of Kentucky, and only a year ago a Hatfield boy and a McCoy girl, members of the old-time clan families, met in class room at Harvard university, and a few weeks ago a staid old mountain minister joined the pair in a happy bond that united the two murderous families and the Angel of the Lord wiped away all the bitterness of the years.

In this vast country of ours, the United States of America, there is properly what might be termed a subdivided love—a love of native state which in no wise interferes with a love of country, but on the contrary makes that love of country the more pronounced, the more satisfying. And no state in all this union has inspired her sons and daughters quite so deeply, quite so lastingly, quite so all-absorbingly a love as has the state of Kentucky. Take

Kentuckians in any section of the world that you may find them, in any circumstances and under any conditions, and there is always apparent the affection which they feel for their native state which finds its quick and hearty outlet in the affection which they evidence toward any fellow Kentuckian whom they may meet. It matters not whether they come from the mountains or the blue grass or the pennyrile. All of them are Kentuckians, with the traditions of Kentucky, with the pride of Kentucky, with the great broad generosity of Kentucky, where the latch-string always hangs on the outside of the door.

That is one of the reasons that 5,000 Kentuckians from all over Kansas and northwestern Oklahoma are asking that another Kentucky picnic be held this year, and that is one of the big reasons why every mother's son of them will come to Wichita on September 1, and bring along with him every member of his family, and it is one of the reasons why the Kentucky picnic will be the biggest event in Wichita this year—just fool Kentuckians who love Kansas, love their native state, and above all love the men and women who hail from Old Kentucky.

Kansas Kentuckians are proud of Kansas as well as their native state. They will tell you that Kansas has 165,879 farms, averaging 275 acres each; that the total value of Kansas farm land and buildings is $2,504,320,108, which exceeds that of 41 other states; that in production of petroleum Kansas ranks fourth among the states, with an annual output more than twice the value of the gold mined in the United States and Alaska in the same period. Only one state has a greater packing industry than Kansas, only two have a greater milling industry, and only three produce more zinc. They will tell you that while first in the production of wheat and other agricultural crops, Kansas is fast becoming an industrial state; that natural gas and cheap electric power are playing a big part in this development. They will tell you that Kansas has the second largest creamery in the United States; that she has averaged more than 100,000,000 bushels of wheat a year for the last 10 years; that her beautiful and stately capital building is the pride of the people. From an architectural standpoint there are few public buildings in America so attractive in the matter of altitude and proportion. They will tell you that there are 8,794 school districts in Kansas, with 18,375 teachers, superintendents and principals; there are 9,326 school buildings and 19,981 school rooms, with a total cost of school buildings of $8,983,912, but still, every so often there comes a feeling around his heart strings and to himself he will say:

"Sing me a song of the sunny South,
One with a sweet refrain;
Sing me a song of Dixie land,
That I may be happy again.
Sing me a sweet Southern melody,
Something of a bye-gone day,
Sing one song for my Old Kentucky Home,
For my Old Kentucky Home far away."

YOUTH CHASES THE GOLDEN HOURS WITH NIMBLE FEET

Old Timers Danced Charleston Forty Years Ago Under the Silvery Moon.

"I've wandered today to the hills, Maggie,
To watch the scenes below,
The creek and the creaking old mill, Maggie,
As we used to long ago."

I have a fairly good sized herd of boys and girls that I call my own, and they are always doing some kind of monkey shine that they call the "Charleston."

Some times when they step off something they think is new and "high falutin' " that has neither time or rhythm, I ask them where they learned it? and they tell me "out at the Heath." So one evening while coming from the oil fields I stopped at the Heath and watched the boys and girls of Wichita—happy sons and graceful daughters—

marking time with nimble feet to music that swept with Orpheus figures every chord of the human heart, and it carried me back to boyhood days when I used to take hold of my true love's hand, touch her waist with my finger tips and glide her through the mazes of a rip-roarin' square dance held in a barn after a day's "huskin' bee," which was common in that neck of the woods at that long ago time.

It carried me back to my old Kentucky home among the hills at the foot of the mountains, where as a boy the happy years sped on as years are wont to do, until we met the heroine of our dreams, and awooing went and sought to toll the fair beauty forth to candy pullings, singing schools, log rollings, and other hilarious gatherings where the youth and beauty of the back districts met to chase the glowing hours with nimble feet.

For more than an hour I sat on the side lines and watched the younger generation "strut their stuff," and I'm here to tell you that they don't know anything about dancing, at all, at all. Some of these evenings when time hangs heavy I am going to look up Jim Maxey and John Gee and Harve Pennington and go out to the Heath and show these latter day boys and girls how to "step it off" to the tune of "The Devil's Dream," and "Old Joe Clark," and a few other old-time tunes that will tickle the toes, and put real devilment into the heels of a boy and girl on the saw dust under the silvery moon.

Of course Jim and Joe and Harve and me are getting along in years, and our joints are a little stiff, but just let two old mountaineers with a corn stalk fiddle and a gourd banjo, reel off a few notes of "Turkey in the Straw," while Jim Maxey "dog trots" to the center of the ring and in a loud and sonorous voice, exclaims: "Salute your lady! Balance all; salute the ladies right and left; everybody dance; swing your partner; balance all; first couple forward and back again; balance all; fourth couple forward and back again; balance all; first lady cast off to the opposite couple, swing your partner, balance all; gentleman balance to right hand lady, swing and balance to opposite lady, swing your partner and half promenade home; balance all;

ladies doce-do, gents you know; first couple to the second, swap your partners, balance to the next and swap all around, balance all and Indian file home; first lady forward and cut the figure eight; first couple balance to fourth couple to the right, steal your neighbor's partner and swing to the left; gents to the right, ladies to the left, Indian file home; honor your ladies and take your seats," I'm thinking that old age and creaky joints would be forgotten, and us old timers could "step it off" in a way that would make young Charleston fans ashamed of themselves.

Or possibly it was a barn dance, commonly known in those days as a "huskin' bee." At the "huskin' bee" the thrifty old farmer with a barn larger than his house, would gather in the corn from the fields, and dump it in one big pile in the middle of the barn. The word would be sent out that Mr. Farmer would entertain with a "huskin' bee" on Saturday afternoon and night, and the younger set would prepare for the occasion like unto Solomon in all his glory. For miles and miles around the countryside would come bucksom young damsels in red and blue calico gowns and linsey-woolsey petticoats with just a peep of white lace occasionally showing between the shoe top and the calico. After the crowd had congregated the names of the girls would be written on a slip of paper, dumped in the feed basket, then the boys would draw a name for his partners. After the partners were selected we circled around that corn pile and tore off the husks with the speed of a sway backed mule on the race track. There was method, too, in our speed, for every time the boy found a red ear he was entitled to the pleasure of kissing his girl, and the lassie was granted the same privilege. I used to slip out to the barn early in the evening, hunt out the red ears and place them in a pile where I could find them when the huskin' started.

Then at night, when the corn was shucked, we cleared away the space in that big barn and the dancing started. And I'm telling you, here and now, that nothing ever seen at the Heath could equal that old-time barn dance. It was at the barn dance that Old Jim waxed sentimental in calling the set, and here is about the way it went:

"Two little ladies side by side, gents come down on the old cow hide; hands in your pockets and backs to the wall, take a chew of tobacco and promenade all; balance all and your partner swing, down the center and bust the ring; ladies forward the gents to meet, swing them ladies clear in the street; gentlemen forward and back ag'in, if you tread the ladies' toes you are darn poor men; shuffle your brogans with your hands on your hips, kiss that lady square on the lips; don't act like an old dead beat, treat your lady and take your seat."

To the boys and girls at the Heath the Charleston is something new, but to Jim and John and Harve and me it's the same old thing that we stepped 40 or more years ago. There is this difference, however, we didn't have any waxed floors and no tented open-air house, and no pumps, and no scissor-tailed coats. We went out in the woods, cleared off the grass under the shade of the trees for two or three hundred feet square, hauled saw dust and bedded down the ring, and all was ready for the fray.

We wore brogan shoes and hickory shirts and jeans or cottonade breeches, and a silk handkerchief for a necktie, and parted our hair in the middle, and later married the girls, and multiplied and replenished the earth. We were just as bad then as our boys and girls are today, and they ain't no more going to the devil than we were. The older folks talked about us just the same as they are talking about the boys and girls of today, and we didn't give a darn any more than the boys and girls of the present age. In the final wind up we'll die and they'll die, but if they have any more fun at the Heath than we had at that barn dance or the saw dust ring in the woods—well, just once again I'd like to turn back old time in its flight, and dance with those same girls in linsey-woolsey, while old Jim Maxey, with a corn stalk fiddle, played:

"Turkey in the straw, boys, Turkey in the straw,
Fetch a piece of rosin, and give the bow a saw,
Drop your knitting Mammy, get the fiddle paw,
And we'll have a little session now of Turkey in the Straw.

"Clear away the kitchen, for we'll have a dance tonight,
Swing your partner gently, and a-stepping mighty light,
Daddy in the corner with the fiddle to his jaw
Everybody's capering to Turkey in the Straw.

"Pigeon-wing and shuffle, and a-stomping on the floor;
Shingles all a-rattling, and latches on the door,
Never any bed-time, nor a-picking any flaw;
Good to die a-dancing to Turkey in the Straw."

JAZZ AGE ETIQUETTE NO IMPROVEMENT OVER OLD TIMES

Rancher Throws the Chicken Bones out at the Door for the Dogs Instead of Laying on Table Cloth.

"I've lived to see the jazz age,
With it's flaming youth and such.
But, Pard, I'm here to tell you,
I haven't gained so much."

I have just read a little booklet entitled "Etiquette of Today," and "it shore has changed since the cowboy days" down in Oklahoma.

The fact is the old-time cowboy has about passed into history, even though the moving pictures still cling to his trappings and attempt to resemble the days when the West was young.

The characteristics of the-old time cowboy, even though he now rides an automobile instead of a broncho, and bows his shoulders to the plow, stay with him, despite the fact that he no longer wears leather collars, spurs, chaps or high heeled boots. His limbs still resemble a pair of calipers and he walks with a peculiar rolling gait, a whole lot like the sailor of the sea. You can tell him by the angle at which he tilts his hat, by the way he handles a plug of tobacco, and his general line of etiquette, which is not altogether in keeping with the jazz age.

The "Etiquette of today" says: "One should not mix one's wardrobe. A coat of one suit and the shirt of another should not be worn together."

In costume the cowboy etiquette differed considerably from the present day. His everyday wearing apparel consisted of a pair of chaps, high heel boots and spurs, but when a woman came into the community, or the boys went to town, Sir Walter Raleigh would have been put to shame when it came to chivalry. It was then that the barber did a rushing business and the towels and soaps in the shacks were worked over time. Sometimes the continued scrubbing and efforts at beautifying themselves left a high water mark just below the ears, but they felt terribly dressed up and usually celebrated the arrival of visitors of the gentler sex, by appearing bedecked in a flaming red bandanna and a new pair of boots.

Two or three years after the first ranches were established in Oklahoma, the men were alone and didn't see a woman for many months, according to the story of my old friend Scott Cummins, who came into Oklahoma with the first white men. One day the report got out that a family had moved in on one of the ranches and all the cowboys went to pay their respects. Profiteering was known in those days as well as later, for some one charged the boys a quarter each to look through the crack in the kitchen wall and watch one of Oklahoma's first white women frying flapjacks. Etiquette of today is to eat in a restaurant where a man fries the fritters.

As time wore on and the settlers began cutting up the big ranches and farm houses began to dot the landscape, the cowboy either went farther west or saw what was coming, grabbed a farm, took off his red bandanna, boots and spurs, and tried to accustom himself to the etiquette of the day, but he had a hard time getting down to cases.

The "Etiquette of Today" says: "A man should not seat himself at the dinner table until his wife is seated." But it would be a hard matter, so Harry Carter tells me, to get one of the old-time cowboys to indulge in such foolishness. Harry is one of the most lovable characters I ever met and I believe has a lot more respect for women than the average man of the West, but he doesn't get this jazz age etiquette of a cowpuncher, after a hard day's work, standing around the table waiting for his wife to sit down. The real wife on a cattle ranch, Harry tells me, don't have any time to sit down at meal time, anyway. It is her duty, after cooking the "chuck," to serve it, and keep the children quiet who have to wait.

Harry also tells me that on one particular occasion, when he was trying to be nice and live up to present day etiquette as he understood it the chicken on the dish was getting low, but having been taught that a cowpuncher was entitled to eat as long as he was hungry, he reached in for a third helping, when a little brat who was hanging around the kitchen door, looking longingly at the table, yelled out; "Don't take it all, Harry." That child's mother, so Harry says, was one of those women whose husband never sits down to the table until his wife is seated.

Another paragraph of "Etiquette of Today" says: "Never place food or waste matter on the table cloth." George Crowell, who now lives in Alva, but at one time lived on a ranch which he still owns, out in the hill country, tells me this is all right, and perfectly appropriate, but what is a fellow to do in one of these city dining rooms where there are no doors and windows that are accessible. Anybody knows, says George, that a little plate of the average size, is not large enough to give a fellow room for a lot of chicken bones when there are other things to eat. Out on the ranch, George says, we always keep a few hound dogs, which are as useful as the cow pony or the lariat. These dogs keep the coyotes away, drive in the cows, chase the jack rabbits out of the garden, and at meal time are always hanging around the dining room door to catch the bones and bread crusts that a fellow would otherwise have to lay on the table cloth. "One old dog on my ranch," George says, "can jump eight feet high and catch the left leg of a yellow legged chicken nine times out of ten when I throw it out at the door, and regardless of etiquette, this is a lot more fun than laying it on the table cloth then wiping your sleeve in it."

"Discussions and unpleasant subjects should never be carried on at the table," says "Etiquette of Today." And I am highly in favor of it. How well do I remember, way back yonder in the good old days of childhood's happy hour, that it was generally at the dinner or supper table that father, with a grave countenance and a shadow of pity in his steel blue eye, used to say: "I want to see you out at the wood shed immediately after supper." And I am here to tell you that cornbread and buttermilk and good old turnip greens lost all their flavor for me at that meal. And, oh, boy! there was real etiquette in the way he handled a bridle rein or a hickory switch, and had he lived to have handled it more I no doubt today would have been a better man.

"Etiquette of Today" also says: "Never spit out a prune, peach or cherry stone while at the table." Evidently the proper mode would be to run out the door and manage some way to dispose of it as you ran. Now, I don't know much about the way to dispose of prune and peach and cherry stones at the table and be in sweet accord with this jazz etiquette, but I do know how, when I was riding herd and we fellows went to town and ate at the restaurant Frank Axtel got rid of a hot potato. Did you ever try to eat a potato boiled with the jacket on?

It is the hottest thing this side of that land where you wear a forked tail and handle everything with a pitchfork. Well, Frank and I and one or two of the other boys drifted into Alva one day and dropped into Wally Ong's cafe along about dinner time, and Wally, among other things, served us potatoes boiled in the jacket. Frank, some time back in the earlier days lost his appetite and found one that belonged to a 'hoss.' He fell onto one of those potatoes like a duck on a dough pie, and got a good, large mouthfull, jacket and all. If you ever tried it you very well know that the longer you chew that kind of a potato the hotter it gets. Well, Frank chewed and chewed, and squirmed and squirmed, and the more he chewed and the more he squirmed the hotter that potato got. He had possibly dreamed of the present day etiquette, and didn't want to spit it out. At last, his mouth a ball of living fire, Frank eased that potato out in his hand, threw it against the wall, and apoligized by saying: "Now damn you blaze!"

Of all the fool things I found in that book on "Present Day Etiquette," the most foolish was the one which said: "No hot drinks should be poured from the cup to the saucer to cool." When I read that I threw up the sponge and was ready to say Oh, Waurika! Oh mamma! Oh! Why do our wives spend such a large portion of our daily wage for saucers if we can't pour our coffee in them to cool? And then, who in the dickens has got the time to pour it back in the cup to drink it? I don't know just what the book of etiquette of today would have you do when you get a mouth full of hot coffee, simply because you are not allowed to pour it into the saucer to cool, but I do know what happened when Herb Gould tried to play etiquette and the coffee was hot as Blixen. A pretty little waitress was serving Herb in George DeFrees' cafe. Herb had been on the range, away from civilization for a long time, and was trying to be as polite as a dancing master. He started to gulp that restaurant coffee down like a Digger Indian gulping down a gourd of grasshopper soup, and it was hot. Herb got tangled up in the workings of his esophagus, and he couldn't swallow and he couldn't spit that coffee out. As a last resort he sputtered and sneezed, and a full sized mouth full of that coffee went right down the neck of that waitress' middy, and there was weeping and wailing and gnashing of teeth. Now, frankly, to avoid another accident of this kind hadn't Herb have better poured that coffee in the saucer to cool? I think he had.

This book on "Etiquette of Today" has not changed in one thing, I am glad to say, and that is the tooth pick, for I read in it: "Toothpicks should not be passed at the table but may be left on the sideboard." When we rode the range we never had toothpicks on the table, any more than we have them today. But Beeler Snyder could take a goose quill and whittle out the finest toothpick that you ever saw. And in addition to picking your teeth with a goose quill pick, you could also clean your finger nails, pick the powder out of tubes of a "cap and ball," and perform many other strange feats that these little wooden fellows that are left on the sideboard won't do.

In another place in this booklet I read: "Pale inks are not liked or approved by the best society." When I read that I was ready to give up the ghost and go out in a blaze of glory, for many a cowboy won his best girl by the simple little stanza "my pen is pore, my ink is pale, my love for you will never fail."

To the old timer I would say, never try out these rules of "Etiquette of Today," for you can't make it. For instance this little book says: "When a gentleman meets a lady and stops to speak with her, it is proper for him to remove his hat and retain it in his hand until she requests him to replace it." Well, I tried this out, and I am still going around with my hat in my hand and that was day before yesterday.

POOR WHITE TRASH

Bill Apperson Was Broke When He Landed in Oklahoma But He Won the Things He Desired in Life by Hard Work and Industry.

In the cattle country in the early days of Oklahoma came many strange people, some to work on ranches for a season, herding and branding cattle, others to build homes and grow up with the country.

Among the vast throngs who made the race into the new country, secured homes and stuck it out through the lean years that followed, was Bill Apperson. When the strip was opened the western section of it was only a desert waste of cattle country, and the little town of Alva only a railroad station and post office.

Back in the Cumberland mountains of Kentucky, Bill was deeply in love with Pearl Henderson, but her parents objected to his attentions on the grounds that he came from a family outside the pale of aristocracy in the neighborhood, commonly that known as "poor white trash."

Bill Apperson was a young man, full of life and ambition, and it cut into his pride, but kindled a fire of determination in his breast that stirred him to fight the game of life and win. He went to the railroad station and bought a ticket West. The destination made little difference to him. He wanted to find a new country where a young man willing to work and save had an equal chance with his more fortunate fellows in the game of life. And the agent routed him to the Oklahoma territory line to join the forces that were racing for homes in a new country.

Having suffered the privations of poverty and been denied the girl he loved, Bill's idea was that money does all things, but he didn't realize that it gives and it takes away; that it makes honest men and knaves, philosophers and fools.

Educated in the common schools of the mountains, he was shrewd, cunning and crafty. He inherited the spirit of the gamble and this was his raging passion. He little realized or cared that every device that suddenly changes money from one person to another, leaving no equivalent, produces individual embarrassment—often extreme misery. Bill, in his days in the mountains was a gambler, and this, added to his family ties, caused old man Henderson to break up the little love affair that wrecked his life.

When Bill landed in Alva it was long before the farmer had turned the country into a land of homes and schools and churches, for few of the men who made the race were able to begin building improvements for several years to come. That section of the country at that time was devoted mostly to cattle raising, and its farm values were not really known.

He had only a few dollars in his pockets when he stepped off the train and viewed the vast expanse of territory before him. His pockets contained all his earthly possessions, but in his breast was a determination to start life anew and rise above the name of "poor white trash"—for love can stir a poor man to greater heights the same as it can tear down a rich man, bringing him to the lowest depths of poverty and shame.

He walked to the depot and learned from the station agent that there was but one job in that section of the world, and that was punching cattle. So it was that he found work on the Cross Bar ranch and soon became a full fledged cow puncher.

Compared with present day slang Bill might have been termed a Ford with a Cadillac engine. His structure was small, but concealed far more force and energy than hundreds of other men who were above the 200 pound mark. He was not an expert at broncho riding, but old Jim Woods, the ranch foreman, fixed him up with some clothes he had around the place, gave him a gentle mount, an old saddle, and told him to work it out for himself. Old Jim was a "queer cuss" but took a liking to Bill and meant to make a real man of the prairies out of him. And Bill needed but little making.

A cattle pony is a mighty nice animal when a fellow is acquainted with his ways, but sometimes to a tenderfoot, like the ways of the heathen Chinee, is peculiar. The old cow pony, the men of the frontier days are sorry to admit, is fast disappearing down the Santa Fe trail, following the Indian and the buffalo toward the setting sun.

Bill's first job was holding the line at a round-up. Hundreds of cattle had been rounded up on the prairie and the fattest steers were being "cut out" for the market. Holding the line means merely to keep the cattle within certain bounds while the cowboys drive the ones selected for the market out of the herd and into the shipping lot, ready to be taken to the railroad and loaded onto the cars.

Bill made it pretty well until an old brindle maverick broke through the line and headed south. The pony knew better what to do than Bill, and in an instant was at the cow's heels. The horses Bill had ridden back home run straight, but that fool cow pony turned when the cow turned, and he plowed up the sand for 20 yards. His heart was all right, but his riding and his luck were bad.

Most every Saturday afternoon the boys of the Cross Bar would ride into Alva and swap yarns and drink booze with the boys from the other ranches, and Bill soon became a leader of the gang. He liked the boys and their ways, and made friends with them all. When pay day came at the end of the month the punchers would have a "little spree," and Bill cheerfully joined in on all that was going on. He was the first to shoot out the street lights of the small town, and the first to interfere when the other boys got too rough with a tenderfoot.

In spite of his pranks and dare-devil nature, Bill worked hard, with always the thought of Pearl Henderson, the girl he left behind, uppermost in his mind. He soon became the favorite of old Jim Woods, as well as the punchers, not only of the Cross Bar ranch, but of all the surrounding ranches. He saved his money, spending only what was necessary for living expenses and to keep in good standing with the boys. He soon began to pick up a cow or two of his own, and each month would add a calf to his growing herd, out of his savings.

Land was not as valuable around Alva in those days as it is now. All a man had to do was to file on a claim, stay by it and buy out his neighbor at the price of a grub stake that would carry the family back to his wife's people.

It was not long, only a few years, until Bill had a little ranch of his own. He made other investments in the little town. His herds grew and it seemed that everything he touched turned to gold. From an inexperienced cow puncher he grew to be a rancher and influential citizen within a few years. He built a fine home on his ranch and longed for Pearl Henderson to adorn it and share his prosperity. Then he would remember his unanswered letters, and sullenly rode his herds, determined in his own soul that she would always be ashamed of him because his parents were, as her father said, "poor white trash." In his mind he felt assured that she had already married some other fellow—some honest farmer boy with whom she had played in her girlhood days—and with his herds and his bank stock and other profitable investments he tried to drive her from his memory; but her image would not vanish.

On the day that Bill Apperson left home for the West, Pearl Henderson placed his picture on her dresser and there it had remained. Never during the years had she encouraged the attentions of any other man, but always remained true to the promise she had made to some day become Bill's wife.

"Woman's love," so I've been told, "is stronger than death. It rises superior to adversity and towers in sublime beauty above the niggardly selfishness of the world. Misfortune cannot suppress it; temptation cannot enslave it; enmity alienate it. It is the guardian angel of the nursery and the sick bed; it gives an affectionate concord to the partnership of life and interest; it ever remains the same, to sweeten existence, to purify the cup of life and the rugged pathway to the grave."

Bill had just ridden home from the little cattle town of Alva and brought back the mail. He was getting a bunch of cattle ready for shipment and it was after supper before he opened the papers. As he scanned the old home sheet he caught a story saying: "Mother Apperson is Dangerously ill."

Bill's mind went back to the days of his childhood he remembered the times when that dear old mother sat by the hearthstone long into the night, working, sewing, mending, that he and the other children—poor white trash—might attend school and look as neat and clean as any other children in the district. He remembered the day when he left home, and the words of that dear old mother as she said: "There'll be a vacant chair at the table when you return." Now that mother was sick, and she hadn't heard from her boy in a dozen years, and didn't even know where he was. And next morning found the first outgoing train taking him back to his old Kentucky home and mother.

Twelve years had wrought but little change in the mountains, and Bill found the same easy going spirit still predominating in the little railroad city as in the old days when he occasionally left his mountain haunts and drove to the city which was the nearest railroad station to his old home. He lost no time, however, in the city, but started across the country to the little inland home town in the hills.

Thirty miles across the country was but a short distance to Bill, for in the wild and woolly West he had learned to make long rides and drives in looking after his business interests; and horses in his country were valued only by the speed they could make and by their endurance.

The little town in the foothills of the mountains, where every family had lived since birth, seldom sees a stranger drive into its midst with a panting, foaming team, and Bill's appearance with his horses almost on a run, caused some of the older inhabitants to stare in wide-eyed amazement.

As he drove into the little village he saw a familiar form coming down the street. He was not sure as he drove past, and his eyes kept wandering back over his shoulder as he slowed down the horses. As the team came to a halt he recognized Pearl Henderson, his old sweetheart. She recognized him, stopped at the corner and stood gazing, her face flushed, her whole form in a tremble and her heart pounding at her breast.

Out of the midst of the past flashes the warning: "O, foolish people, that have eyes to see and see not." More than 25 centuries have rolled round since Jeremiah on a hillside in Judeah uttered this searching phrase, and time has added but little wisdom to the man and the maid.

Old man Apperson and old man Henderson were playing marbles in the middle of the street with other inhabitants that made up the population of the little town, and were engaged in a friendly quarrel as to who could knock the middler the most times, straight, when they were boys and their eyes were good. On a row of boxes the village cut-up was betting a Methodist deacon that it would take a circling buzzard 12 minutes to "pass yon gray cloud in the heavens." Small boys were turning up large stones in the court house yard looking for fish bait.

Down in Oklahoma Bill Apperson rides among his herds and meets with the bank directors in the city of Alva. He has served a term in the legislature and refused the nomination of his party for the state senate. He prefers the quietude of his home and family to the devious ways of party politics.

When he returns at night from looking after his herds or from a business meeting in the city, Pearl meets him at the gate, and with arm around her waist they waltz up the path to a home where peace, prosperity and happiness are the chief characteristics and in which Pearl reigns with the grace of a queen.

In the evening, in the coziest corner of the room Pearl rocks little Jack to sleep and croons the same old songs that in older days were sung to the children by the colored mammies in her old Kentucky home:

Don't you weep my honey, don't you cry no more,
  Mammy's gwine to hold her boy—
All the little white trash rolling on the floor,
  Mammy's gwine to hold her boy.

TALES FROM OLD KENTUCKY TOLD BY A NATIVE SON

Shanghai Cloyd Chases His Steers; Uncle Jim Brown Marries the Widow.

"Take me back to old Kentucky,
  To the state where I was born,
Where the corn is full of kernels,
  And the Colonels full of corn;
Where the lassies and the horses
  Are but terms for grace and speed
And the whisky and the statesmen,
  Both are noted for their bead."

Down in Kentucky where I come from there is a little town where old men smoke the pipe of peace in shirt sleeves and contentment, and they call it Tompkinsville.

Thirty years ago when I lived there the male inhabitants lived a quiet, care free life, doing the best they could to eat their pound of tobacco and drink their quart of coffee each day.

All their lives they chose the smoothest path. Down hill or on the level they sought only the route that presented the fewest obstacles and required the least effort.

My earliest recollections are of Shanghai Cloyd. "Shang," as he was familiarly known, was mad at the world, and a mad man's an uncomfortable thing to have around, even though he is not mad at you. Four years in the Union army, including the hell horrors of prison and other places too numerous to mention, had somewhat impaired the old man's health. His physical condition grated on his mind, until he seldom opened his mouth save to take in liquor and tobacco and let out oaths and saliva. His wrinkled features seldom vibrated into a smile, but occasionally, when his friends expected him to break out in a storm on the wings of which rode death, the old man would see the funny side and make a caustic remark that would bring laughter to the crowd. His favorite occupation was hauling wood to the little town from his farm along Mule creek, where scrubby oak grew in rank profusion, with a yoke of mooley steers.

Dr. Duncan had returned from medical school at Louisville and brought back a sheepskin and a bottle of "hokey-pokey," the first time the new medicine had ever been seen in Tompkinsville. When "hokey-pokey" comes in contact with man or beast it sets them almost crazy for a few minutes, with a curious freezing sensation. It was tried out on various cats and dogs around the town, much to the delight of the goods box whittlers who infested the streets.

One day old man Cloyd came to town with the steers and the village cut-up sprinkled a few drops of "hokey-pokey" along their backs, and the steers went over the hill at about the same rate of speed a Bohunk dishwasher turns the corner in dodging the police. Some one explained to old man Cloyd the cause of the steers' swift pace, expecting and hoping to see a general town fight, in which I would come out all mangled and torn, but with a frown on his face that resembled a powder keg, needing only a spark to set it off, the old man said:

"Put some of that stuff on me, I've got to ketch them cattle."

Uncle Jim Brown seemed to me to be smart enough to be high and important in the world, but he wasn't. For twenty years he tilled his little farm and spring always found him battling for bread. Along with raising chickens and pigs. Uncle Jim was raising two feeble-minded children that he had to keep chained to the wall. He rode over the country in the winter months and peddled tobacco and a line of patent medicines. At the time I first knew Uncle Jim he was a widower, longing for a wife. In his rounds over the country he found a buxom widow of forty summers who was also longing for a mate. One day he surprised his friends by going to the parson's with the widow, and there in the presence of God and man, making her his lawful spouse.

After the ceremony they rode over the mountain to Uncle Jim's little farm. From a high peak overlooking the homestead the widow sat in silence and satisfaction as Uncle Jim pointed out his possessions. They rode down to the house, dismounted at the "style" and the new bride went on the inside to inspect her future habitation.

Horror seemed to possess her as she entered the door, and turning to the old man with the fires of lightning burning in her eyes, she demanded:

"Why didn't you tell me you had these two idiots before I married you?"

Without batting an eye Uncle Jim replied:

"Why didn't you ax me?"

William Kelly was the last thing in careless abandon. He was a descendant of one of the wealthiest and most aristocratic families of Tompkinsville—the Kellys,—but lived on a "lime kiln" farm some 20 miles back in the hills. No human being could describe his appearance when he drifted into town to visit his friends and relatives, who by the way, were not looking for him. He wore a miscellaneous assortment of gents furnishing goods. Nails and thorns took the place of buttons, and his costume was coarsely patched beyond recognition of the original fabric.

Lem Kelly was the oldest son of one of the aristocratic families of the town—families that were sometimes termed just a little bit stuck up. Lem was a conspicuous character around the streets, like unto the boys of today who stand on the corner and feel wise and smart, and do and say smart things. Smith Kelley was Lem's father, and the biggest and most aristocratic man in the town.

William was leaning against a lamp post at the edge of the street when young Lem spied him. After looking him over for some time and drawing a crowd of street loafers around him, he approached William with the remark:

"Stranger, I don't want to say anything about you, but I have a curiousity just to know who you are?

William happened to know Lem, and calmly and serenely he replied: "Why, Lemuel, I'm your cousin William Kelly. Where is Uncle Smith?"

Among my most sacred recollections of Tompkinsville is Aunt Amanda Coulter. As there was no newspaper in the little town, Aunt Amanda acted as news bearer and kept the village posted on the happenings of the day. She lived at the outskirts of the town but visited over the village regularly and informed the inhabitants of the happenings in the village and surrounding community. The last time I remember having seen Aunt Amanda she visited my mother and gave this bit of neighborhood news:

"How many chickens you got, Margie? Yesterday evening mine footed up an even hundred, but two or three died last night from cholera. The yellow-legged Brahmas grow amazingly. There ain't no chickens that scratch dirt atop this earth can come up to these corn-fed fries. I don't pin my faith on incubators, neither; give me the old-fashion way of raising chickens and babies. There's John Botts' wife bringing up their baby by the clock. He slops, eats and cries by the time of day. Mary says that singing and rocking babies to sleep has gone out of style with paragoric and peppermint tea.

"Mary, says I, babies are older style than anything I know of. If I remember they occurred back in Biblical times and you are losing heap of pleasure and comfort trying to fit new notions to such old style things as babies.

"Had you heard about the new baby at Will Anderson's? Mother and child doing well, and the boy looks just like its father. Yes, born yesterday night, when the first blue snow fell. I never was superstitious, but I do feel sorry for this little fellow. You know it's not good luck to be born on Wednesday, anyway, and then, too, the dog howled all night before the baby was born.

"Jim Vibbert's Holstein cow, you know the one he bought at that sale up at Glasgow, last February—well, she's got a brindle calf, and she was guaranteed to him to be a full blood.

"Hear that Bill Williams, the new hired man over at John Snell's, is shining up to Maud Huffman a bit. I tell you what, if I was old Charley Huffman no hired man that come from I don't know where, would be flirting around with my daughter.

"That reminds me. There'll be preaching at the Baptist church Sunday evening at early candle light. 'Tis a Baptist or a Cambellite, I don't remember which, but it don't make much difference if a man's got the tact and nerve and faith to give the message it really don't make much difference.

"Well, I must hurry along and get the mail, and get back home. I see a little cloud rising over yonder in the skies and it might rain before nightfall."

There were many queer characters back in the mountains of dear old Kentucky, and I loved them all, but I left after "Dow" Copass told me.

Man that is born in Kentucky is of but feud days and full of virus. He fisheth, fiddleth, cusseth and fighteth all the days of his life. He shunneth water like a mad dog and drinketh much good whiskey. He riseth from his cradle and goeth forth to seek the scalp of his grandsire's enemy, and he bringeth home in his carcass the ammunition of his neighbor's wife's cousin's father-in-law, who avengeth the deed.

Verily his life is uncertain and he knoweth not the hour he will be dispatched. He goeth forth on a journey half shot and returneth again to his habitation on a litter, full of buckshot. He riseth in the night to let the cat out, and it requireth a doctor three days to extract the lead from his body. He goeth forth in joy and gladness, and cometh back in scraps and fragments. He calleth his fellow man a liar, and is himself filled with shot and scrap iron, even to the fourth generation. A cyclone bloweth him into the arms of his neighbor's wife, and his neighbor's wife's husband bloweth him into the arms of Father Abraham before he hath time to explain. He emptieth a demijohn into himself, and a shot gun into his enemy, and his enemy's son lieth in wait for him on election day, and lo! the coroner ploweth up a forty-acre field to bury the remains of that man.

"Yes, take me back to old Kentucky,
  Let me hear the pistols pop,
See the pigs and politicians
  With their snouts eye deep in slop.
Take me back to those blue mountains,
  Where they argue points with lead;
But you needn't rush the matter—
  Take me back when I am dead."

OUT OF TOBACCO

John Bedford's Grandfather Lived to Be 105 Years Old Chewing Tobacco, so He Told Me, But I Have Found the Same Remedies Are Not Good for Every Fellow.

A few nights ago Victor Murdock told me: "Every time I am out of tobacco you are out, too," and this started the argument. Victor is editor-in-chief of The Eagle and I am only a reporter, so he won the argument.

A long time ago when I was a mere slip of a boy, John Bedford told me his grandfather chewed tobacco and lived to be 105 years old. Then it was I started out to live to a ripe old age, but the first chew I took almost killed me; in fact for several hours I was sick enough to die, and wouldn't have cared much at the time if I had. John may have told me the truth. I don't know, for since I had the flu I have learned that what is good for one man is not always good for the other. But I do know that it would have been a good thing for me if throughout the years I had been forced to say to every other fellow: "Every time I am out of tobacco you are out, too."

Down in Kentucky where I came from old men smoke the pipe of peace in shirt sleeves and contentment. Some of them walk on their hind legs and chew tobacco like humans, but right there the resemblance ceases, while others have all the characteristics and refinements of the human being, and still chew tobacco. For years they have met life as it comes and the odds don't worry them any. They raise enough wheat to bread them, enough hogs to make their meat, and enough corn to feed the live stock and have corn bread three times a day, and the time never comes when one of them can say to his neighbor: "Every time I am out of tobacco you are out, too."

When I was a boy, chewing tobacco was an art. Men practiced it the same as their sons practiced dancing and playing seven-up. It took a real man to chew that Kentucky long green, but everybody chewed, and Kentuck turned out such families as the Lincolns, the Clays, the Marshalls and other like national characters. Old men chewed their tobacco and spit their juice, but they tried hard to keep their boys from chewing.

Whether they thought it an evil habit, not good in the sight of the Lord, or wanted to save tobacco, I never knew, but it is a fact that we kids had to do most of our early chewing out behind the barn, and if dad caught us there was the devil to pay. Tom Marshall was one of the kids in my set who learned to chew tobacco behind the barn along about the same time. One day Tom's father came around the barn unexpectedly, and caught Tom and me biting a hunk out of one of his favorite twists that he had been aging for years. Old man Marshall flew into a rage, and began to heap abuse on Tom's head. But Tom settled the argument in a characteristic Marshall way when the old man gave him time to talk. Tom merely said: "Don't upbraid me, father; it is the only inheritance I ever received." And from that day on Tom's father and Tom were never out of tobacco at the same time and no member of the Marshall household was ever able to say: "Every time I am out of tobacco you are out, too."

When I first came to work on The Eagle nine years ago, Farmer Doolittle was a conspicuous character around the shop. Farmer loved his tobacco as well as any Kentuckian I ever saw, and consumed large quantities of the weed each and every day. Farmer always kept a goodly stock of the best brands in his desk, and never during the years that he lived, after I arrived here, did he ask any human being for a chew of tobacco. But Farmer had a friend who did not keep himself so well supplied with the long green as did Farmer. In fact, this particular friend seldom bought any tobacco. He didn't chew very much, but what little he did chew he worked Farmer for it. One day this particular gentleman, having asked Farmer for more than the customary amount of chews during the day, apologized by saying: "I don't chew enough tobacco to justify me to buy any." And Farmer, who was wise in the ways of men, answered and said unto him: "You are wrong, my friend, you don't buy enough tobacco to justify you to chew any." Both Farmer Doolittle and this particular fellow were around The Eagle office together for a good many years after this, and during the remainder of the years no man was ever again able to say to this particular fellow: "Every time I am out of tobacco you are out, too."

John Bedford, the man who first gave the impression that I ought to chew tobacco, was the most graceful tobacco chewer I ever saw. John seasoned and twisted his own tobacco, and it was the most beautiful brown to be conceived of. He knew the art of preparing tobacco as no other man in the Kentucky hills knew it. He carried it in a hog's bladder made especially for the purpose, and it would make most any fellow's mouth water to see John take a twist of long green out of that hog's bladder, open a sharp bladed knife, cut off a hunk and place it properly in his jaw. When I was a little tot, possibly eight or nine years old, I watched John Bedford take a chew of tobacco, and never a time did I see him do it but that I longed for the time to come when I would be a man, and like John Bedford, could clip off a chew of long green as gracefully as a dancing master, and hit a cuspidor in the far corner of the room. John never owned much of this world's goods. He allowed as how sporadic wealth paid dividends only in tears, while a chew of good tobacco pays dividends in contentment, and the man who is content is most happy. Possibly it was for this reason that no man could ever truthfully say to John Bedford: "Every time I am out of tobacco you are out, too."

Uncle Jim Brown was another character of the tobacco chewing section of Kentucky, and a character unto himself Uncle Jim was. Uncle Jim raised tobacco and sold it over the countryside. During the long stretches of the winter season he would cure and twist the long green, and during the spring and summer would travel from house to house, and from town to town, and peddle the twisted product. In packing his goods for market he would put two twists on a string and sell it for a dime, or six twists on a string and sell it for a quarter. Uncle Jim had his own peculiar ideas about life and men in general, and while the unions had not been organized in that section of the country at that time, had they been Uncle Jim would possibly have been president of the tobacco salesmen's union. Tompkinsville, the county seat town of the county in which Uncle Jim lived, had possessed no railroads and no banks until Uncle Jim reached a ripe old age. Then a bank was organized, and Dora Smith came down from the city to act as cashier of the new organization back in the foothills of the Cumberland. Uncle Jim came to town with his poke of tobacco and wandered around to the bank.

I had always been a customer of his, and immediately bought a string of his twists. After I had made the purchase for 25 cents, I introduced Uncle Jim to Mr. Smith. Uncle Jim explained to Smith the good qualities of his tobacco, and Smith told him he would take a string. Uncle Jim fished out a nice string of the twists from his poke, handed it to Smith, with a request for 50 cents. Smith demurred and said: "Why, Mr. Brown, you just sold Eubank a string of the same tobacco for 25 cents, I saw you make the sale, and can't understand why you charge me 50 cents?" "Simple enough, simple enough," replied Uncle Jim. "You're a banker."

Dora Smith bought tobacco from Uncle Jim for many years after this, and there never was a time thereafter when one of the patrons of the bank could say to Mr. Smith: "Every time I am out of tobacco you are out, too."

Dora Smith and John Bedford, however, were exceptions to the rule. I worked by the side of Bill Laird for five or more years, and some times I ran out of tobacco, and I noticed, like Victor Murdock, that every time I was out of tobacco Laird was out, too. Bill was a philosopher, a student of human nature, and a good judge of tobacco. He preferred a cob pipe to a chew, but was an expert at both. When Bill got his pipe lit, and it puffed free, he could tell you a lot of things about the successes of this life, and how to accomplish them, although a living was a hard thing for him to make. On one occasion when fate had not been very kind to either of us, and we had been forced to hustle tobacco for two or three days as best we could, owing to the failure of the Saturday night pay check to make connections, a delinquent subscriber dropped in and paid a few dollars on subscription. The editor was out, and Bill and I took the money and invested in a goodly supply of tobacco. With our new purchase and new pipes well filled, as we sat with our feet on the desk causing blue smoke to spiral in the clear morning air, Bill told me: "The ingredients of success are 40 per cent bluff, 20 per cent luck, 10 per cent ability, and the remainder a pipe of good tobacco." I learned this lesson from Bill Laird, and I learned it well, and it is only on occasions when I am dead broke, like the other night, when Victor Murdock can say to me: "Every time I am out of tobacco you are out, too."

Any man can dance when the band is playing, but it takes a good man to keep on rocking when the music stops and he's out of tobacco, and life is a dangerous trip from the cradle to the grave if there is nothing to chew or smoke along the route, for the average man don't sit and think; he sits and chews or smokes. Joe Black was of the general run of fellows. I have seen Joe sitting at a rickety table, his future looming up like a constant succession of rainy days and leaky shoes and hope deferred to make the heart sick, but if his pipe puffed free, whether or not his belly was full, he was happy. Joe was a tobacco chewer as well as a smoker, back in the nineties, when the skirts of American womanhood still swept the avenues. Joe's aim with a mouth full of tobacco juice was not always as good as his circle of rings. He would stand on the street corner, take a chew of long green, and start rhapsodizing. And sometimes the womanhood, sweeping the streets, would cast menacing frowns in Joe's direction as they passed along the street where he was chewing. He was a queer cuss and you could never tell whether he'd land in the lap of riches or the north room of the nearest jail, but there was one thing you could always bet on, that no man could ever say to Joe: "When I am out of tobacco you are out, too."

Ever since the apple-eating episode in the Garden of Eden, man has used tobacco in some form or another, and I guess he always will, and there are some I know, who I truly believe when they are patted in the face with a spade, will appear at the pearly gates with a pipe in their mouth, for these fellows, if they have enough to eat and a place to sleep and their pipe pulls free, are content, like unto a complacent, good-humored bull in a clover field.

But of all things sad, all things lonely, all things demoniacal, it is this class of men when one is forced to say to the other: "When I am out of tobacco you are out, too."

Victor Murdock is my boss. He is editor-in-chief of The Eagle. In my honest opinion he is among the greatest writers and deepest thinkers in America today. His editorials in The Eagle sparkle with wit, humor and fact and are copied in the leading newspapers of the nation. His associations with the boys around the shop are inspiring and pleasant, but I can't help but wonder just what kind of a fellow Victor Murdock would be if too often he had to say, not only to me, but to everybody else in the wide, wide world: "Every time I am out of tobacco you are out, too."

BALLOON BREECHES NOTHING NEW TO "US OLD TIMERS"

They Were in Style When Our Wives Wore Long Skirts, Big Sleeves and Bangs, and We Married 'Em.

"Gimme the guy with a straight-forward eye,
  And a grip that'll hurt your hand,
With a tongue that he uses but never abuses;
  A mind that can understand.
The boy that'll brag of his mother, by gad,
  And who thinks of all women the same;
Who toils with a smile, a lad you can't rile;
  One who puts his whole heart in the game."

How many of you old timers, whose shadows are falling to the west, remember the old-fashioned boy that went in his shirt tail until 10 or 11 years old, that being about the only garment he possessed during the summer months? He could step up to an old rail fence and if he could hang his hand on the top rail, he would step back and leap over it and his shirt tail would make a kind of fluttering noise as he went over.

How many of you old timers remember the old-fashioned boy and girl that became one in wedlock and went just across the spring branch from the old folks on the slope of the hill and built a house under the shadow of the old tree and raised a family and lived for God and humanity?

When I see my boy and your boy standing on the street corner in front of a drug store, wearing a pair of balloon pantaloons and thinking he is all dressed up in something new, it amuses me. I have grand children—two of the finest little rascals on earth—and I was married in a pair of big-legged breeches. They measured 22 inches around, and I guess I looked like a toad frog in a hail storm, me measuring only five feet two inches tall. I thought at that time, just like the boys think today, that I was a Lilliputian dandy.

I introduced the style back in my little home town many years ago. It was the first pair of "Father Hubbards"—that was what we called them then—ever worn in the little mountain town and they attracted considerable attention.

Uncle Delbert Chism, one of the old timers of that day, looked me over from head to foot, while he chewed his tobacco ruminatively, the juice of which he spat with admirable skill across his white beard and at a designated mark within sporting range, and then remarked:

"Eubank, if you'll take them things off I'll crawl all through them."

When the style came back and our boys called it new, I immediately went into a pair of balloons, but I soon discovered that youth is youth and with it age cannot compete for favor in bright eyes.

My wife, too, dressed in style when she was young, but the styles she wore then, like the Indian and the buffalo, have passed on toward the setting sun never to return.

When we were married she wore big sleeves and long skirts and bangs, and alongside of her a royal flush made a poor showing. Sitting among the crowd at our play parties and church gatherings, to me she looked like a lily among a muck-heap, and no silk stockinged girl of today is as beautiful to me as gingham and the garden gate waiting for a lover strong and true.

I wasn't what a woman might wish for a husband in many ways, but she took me and made of me a man, and now, sometimes, I think just her and my pipe and slippers, under a fan, is all I want in life. Then I put on those balloon breeches and I think, well, I may be speeding toward the end, but I'm not crawling on my hands and knees.

When I was a boy, and she was a girl, I sometimes think, we had a lot more fun than the boys and girls have today. We played "snap-up." This was the greatest game of them all. A girl and a boy stood in the center of the room holding hands at full arms length. The boy, whose turn it was, had the privilege of "snapping up" the girl of his choice, then running around the boy and the girl in the center of the room until she caught him or her time limit expired. If the boy made the circle five times without being caught, he won, and had the glorious privilege of kissing the girl who "snapped him up."

Oh boy! we kids would run like blue racers, and as a rule the sweet little girl didn't try very hard to catch us. Then it was the girl's turn to "snap-up" her boy. If he caught her before she made the circle of five he had the privilege of kissing her. I don't think I ever failed to catch but one girl in the game of "snap-up," and I remember her distinctly. She was getting along in years, and wanted to be snapped up for life. I caught her the first time, and discovered she had eaten garlic for supper. On the second occasion when she "snapped me up" I had a knocked down hip, a sore toe and a broken ankle and every other conceivable thing to impede speed.

It was along about this time that the doctors went in for the germ craze, and announced that kissing was dangerous in the extreme, a veritable flaming sword; that the fairest maiden's lips were loaded with microbes, her kiss a Judas osculation, betraying the sighing swain who dares to browse upon her dewey lips, to well nigh certain death. It may be true as the doctor told us, that death lurked in the lover's kiss like a yellow-jacket in a hoss apple but we continued to play "snap-up" just the same.

When this edict of the doctors went forth, I was afraid my girl would pass up our play parties, so I wrote her: "The learned physician tells us there is danger in a kiss, disease and death may reach us through that avenue of bliss. But when a fellow gets a chance to kiss a pretty maid, he's very apt to say, O, darn the doctor, who's afraid."

I kindly doubt, however, if it would be wise for the boys of today to play our old-time game of "snap-up," for since old man Volstead created a Sahara desert in America a good remedy for painter's colic is not always at hand.

As I remember at this time, we heard, just as we hear today, that age old story, "our girls are going to the devil." We had as many, or more, I think, of those chronic old brothers and sisters whose ideas were to make everyone else as miserable as themselves. To these dear people our play parties were placed under the ban, and every daughter of Eve who allowed herself kissed in a "snap-up" game was going to the devil in a hand basket. To these old timers the young people were expected to do their courting with a solemnity befitting the makings of contracts in a coffin factory. They would turn the sunshine of the heart into rainy days and leaky shoes and hope deferred to make the heart sick.

But the girls of our day rebelled at their foolishness and gradually the dark clouds fled from the hills and the dismal mists from the valleys, for these damsels married sturdy sons of good ancestry and proceeded to follow in the footsteps of him who said "multiply and replenish the earth."

It matters not whether it's your sweetheart of today or your father's sweetheart of yesteryear, they all sum up about the same, and always, in the midnight of man's distress the sanctuary of her arms appeals to him as the one refuge where he is safe from the batterings of an unkind world—but a man is sometimes liable to be mistaken. Men bow to her beauty and wit—then pay, as they have done since Adam was driven out of the Garden of Eden.

"Oh, foolish men, that have eyes to see, and see not." More than 20 centuries have rolled round since Jeremiah, on a hillside in Judea uttered this searching phrase, and men and women have changed but little since that time.

The youth, crazy over the maiden, as was his father, still exclaims: "a more lovely creature since the days of Helen, was never born for the undoing of man."

Between the ages of 15 and 20 the woman of today like the woman of yesteryear, thinks she is innocent, and therefore dangerous; at 20 she thinks she is sophisticated and is therefore dangerous; between 20 and 30 she is misunderstood—but your father never got that far, and neither will you, for no woman ever gets that old.

"So gimme a Miss who values her kiss,
Who has time for much else besides curls,
The feminine kind with the practical mind
Who stands pretty solid with girls,
Who can lure me to lunch, who can mix with the bunch,
Who can cry when the thing calls for tears,
Who can fondle a baby, and dream a bit, maybe,
And be a good pal through the years."

WHEN KENTUCKIANS GO PICNICKING IN HOME STATE

Grandma Stroud Sells Cider While the Male Inhabitants "Swap Hosses" and Have a Good Time.

"The young folks roll on the little cabin floor,
All merry, all happy and bright.
Bye and bye hard times comes a knocking at the door,
Then my old Kentucky home good-night."

The Kentuckians are going to have an old-time Kentucky picnic, and if it runs true to form there'll be work for the coroner to do.

Since the days when our Ayran ancestors took their women and children, their cattle and horses, and started from Central Asia to conquer new homes with the sword, the roving instinct has been our heritage—the wanderlust in our blood.

Back in the years a whole lot of Kentuckians followed in the wake of their forefathers from Asia and wandered into Kansas to conquer new homes by beating Uncle Sam, the grasshoppers and the hot winds in the game of "stick it out or starve," and now they are going to get together for an old time frolic.

Some of the oldest old-timers stuck it out and proved up their claims. Some came later and bought their land for a song. Others settled in the cities and farmed the farmer, but they all learned that while their women attended bargain sales and the men played "seven-up," the question of getting something for nothing remained unsolved.

They stayed on, for every man of them wanted a home, but many times the good wife wondered what they were going to do when they got restless, and the sun went down slowly, and they got homesick sitting on their own front porch. But still they stayed on, for it was a man's country where they think in leagues instead of city blocks and neighbors were not so many but that every stranger was a friend—and they hailed from Kentucky, where they learned the hospitality that "come weary to any man's door and his house is yours."

These old-timers didn't sit around, either, waiting for the ravens to feed them. They went out on the prairies, caught a jack rabbit and had a good Sunday dinner.

Some of them settled in towns and years of dyspepsia and business killed all their Kentucky hospitality, but they came as near smiling as their tortured stomachs would permit, when it was announced that they were going to have an old-time Kentucky picnic.

I don't know just how this old-time Kentucky picnic will turn out, but if some of the Hatfields and McCoys, or the Howards and the Bakers happen to come together and remember the old county court days the first Monday in each month, when all the neighborhood bullies met and tested their skill in blacking eyes and kicking shins and bitting thumbs, the guardian angel that is watching the outcome of this get-to-gether Kentucky crowd, is more than likely laughing over the ways of men, for I have heard it said that back in Kentucky in the old days

"The feud man hides in the corner of the fence,
And waits for a shot at his foe,
And a foeman's soul goes a kiting to the hence,
To the land where they don't shovel snow."

Back in Kentucky they have many different kinds of picnics, for the word picnic, in its common and accepted sense, covers most everything where there is fun and something to eat.

The first Monday in each month, in the little county seat town where I was first watched by an old negro mammy for a couple of days to see whether I would cry or bark, was county court day, and this day was a picnic for every mae inhabitant of the county. They all come to town on county court day and mingled in business and blissful inebriation, and ate their dinners in the grocery store, lining up alongside a board counter and munching cheese, or oysters or sardines, which was helped along in its onward course by a tumbler or so of sod corn, made in a moonshine still especially for the occasion.

A small number in the crowd that came to town on that day had business at the court house, but the great majority come to "swap hosses." One particular "hoss swapper" that I remember, was Jim Dunham. The day before the first Monday Jim could always be seen in town purchasing a keg of soda and a pound of ginger, and on the eventful morning of the First the streaks of dawn would see old Jim coming down the street with a string of five or six "skates," which in former years had been horses, each haltered to the other, their tails held high—not from sheer ambition, but on account of the ginger—their sides pouched out—not from hay and corn, but soda—a veritable bone yard blowed and gingered up like balloon ties, on a second-hand Ford. Any "hoss" in his string could have been fittingly described as

"One old "hoss," round as a ring,
Eighteen years old, 19 in the spring;
One eye out, one eye glass,
Two white feet, a spot in the face;
Sides bulged out, tail caved in—
A darn good "hoss" for the fix he's in."

and all day long Jim Dunham and the hundreds of others of his profession would gallop and trot and walk, and run the old skates up and down the street, "swappin' hosses," sometimes even, sometimes giving or getting anything from ten cents to $2.50 "to boot."

On one occasion I saw Jim make what to me was the most amusing trade of his life. Jim traded "hosses" with Charley Thomas, another "hoss swapper," and he received as "boot" in the trade a twist of "home spun" tobacco, a Jew's harp, a two-bladed pocket knife and two drinks of whisky, and in my opinion Jim got the better "hoss" of the two, for in less than an hour after the trade the "hoss" died of "soda colic." And to add to his good or bad luck, Jim landed in jail for being drunk, for at that time, back in old Kentucky, it wasn't soft drinks that men waved on the jockey track.

The regular "honest-to-goodness" picnic, however, was of a different nature. Every community had its picnic grounds and every so often it was announced by word of mouth that a big picnic would be staged at Caney Ford, or Mud Lick or Vibbert's Ridge. Then it was that the entire family turned out. They went in buggies, lumber wagons, steer wagons, horse back and a-foot. The whole herd from grandma to the infant in swaddling clothes took in these picnics. For days ahead of time they cooked chicken and bread, hog and hominy, sorghum molasses and corn pone, and they brought it along and spread it on the ground and at noon and at night the hungry horde swooped down on that "slumgullion" in an ospinarious fashion like unto a hungry coyote on a hen roost. And they told war stories and parlor stories, and sang songs, and drank mintjuleps, and at nightfall the old and decrepit went joyously home to their squalid cabins, while the younger set lingered behind as the Kentucky moon hung like a silver slipper over the purple stretches of the night; the perfume of summer flowers drifting in from the blue grass fields to mingle gently with the aroma of wild honeysuckle hanging in a heavy network over the tall trees, under which the boys and girls—the one handsome and the other beautiful—sipped a cool liquid from long glasses in which fresh mint was floating—but it was red lemonade, a rare treat in that section of old Kentucky.

And old Aunt Amanda Stroud was always there with her little dog cart, drawn by a yoke of oxen or a pair of aged mules. Aunt Amanda had passed the three score and ten mark, and her years in the kitchen had improved her culinary arts until no woman in the whole countryside could equal her in baking ginger cakes. And Grandpa Stroud, having grown up in a country frequented by moonshine stills, could make the best apple cider of any man in the land.

Aunt Amanda sat on a rickety stool by the side of her dog cart and sold a glass of cider and a ginger cake for five cents, and every time I think of it I long to go back to Old Kentucky, for as I remember at this time

> "The prettiest girl I ever saw,
> Was sucking cider through a straw."

and I married her and have lived happily ever afterwards.

We had the neighborhood bullies, too, who invariably attended these picnics. One I remember in particular was Mose Belcher of the Rock Bridge neighborhood. Mose was noted all over the country for his mean fighting qualities, and one of the tricks we younger boys used to perform at the picnic was to climb a tree and watch the fights after Mose landed on the grounds. He always picked his man—one a little smaller or for some reason or other he felt assured that he could whip, and he always succeeded. The quiet, law-abiding citizens dodged Mose, and most of the bullies were afraid of him.

It was along in the middle of the afternoon when Mose lit on the grounds and started looking for trouble. He spied Jack Maxey dancing with one of the belles of the country, and picked him as his prey. Jack had "been away at school," and returned just a little more polished than the rest of us boys, but he was one of our crowd, just the same. Along with his school studies Jack had taken a few lessons in athletics, and was a star member on the foot-ball team.

Mose edged up close to the dancing ring and began to make remarks about the looks of the little lassie Jack was dancing with. Jack listened to these remarks for some little time, then slowly pulled off his coat and handed it to one of the boys. Mose saw him as he went out of his coat and lunged at him, expecting to swallow him like a cat devouring a mouse, but a fellow is sometimes liable to be mistaken. Jack, who was a much smaller man, ducked under his arm like a bantam and punched him in the pit of the stomach so that he doubled up with a groan. Before Mose could straighten up Jack was on him, fighting like the wildest fury that ever trod the hills of the back district. Mose dealt thundering blows that sometimes landed and sent Jack reeling, and sometimes he missed, and went plunging into the scattering crowd with the impetus of his own force. Jack could not strike with one-half of Mose's force, but he could land three blows to his one. Jack ducked, danced and dodged. For the first 10 or 20 minutes he endured fearful punishment. Then Mose's breath commenced to whistle through his teeth, when Jack had only begun fighting. He saw an opening and forgot all laws or rules of the prize ring and drove the toe of his shoe into Mose's stomach until he doubled up and fell heavily. Then Jack stomped and kicked him until the crowd pulled him away.

Each bully in the neighborhood always had his backers, and they followed along with him to cheer him on and help in the fray if it became necessary, but in this particular instance Mose's henchmen didn't have a chance, for Jack's friends were on the side lines keeping them back.

After the fight was over one of Mose's henchmen peered through the crowd, looked Jack over, and inquired:

"Say, you dude, over there, can we come and get him?"

Thus ended the career of a noted neighborhood bully, for it was the last fight Mose Belcher ever had. I heard later that he settled down and became a decent citizen, and I can't help but wonder just how many of the old-timers that will be at this Kentucky picnic have seen similar circumstances back in the old home state.

I am heartily in favor of the old-time Kentucky picnic, for how well do I remember that back in old Kentucky on these occasions

"The stone jug rises to kiss the waiting lips,
While the up-turned eyes gladly play
On the soft blue skies of the sunny, sunny south,
In my old Kentucky home far away."

A WEEK OF FUN WHEN I WAS A BOY

War With Roman Candles and Shooting Fire Crackers Was Fun But Mother's Stories Most Enjoyed.

Today, Christmas, 1926, is only a memory, but it brought joy and gladness, to many youngsters in Wichita, and perhaps all over the land.

Of all our annual holidays and festivals Christmas is the most joyful. It is the festival which commemorates the lowly birth of Christ, the foundation of the religion of love and peace, and while grown men and women sometimes look on the serious side of the Christmas celebration, to the little folks it is a day of receiving and rejoicing.

While in every section of the city the merry shouts and peals of laughter from the little folks could be heard, I couldn't help but wonder if these younger folks, in this day of wealth and jazz, with all their finery and plenty, got as much fun out of the Christmas holiday as "when you and I were young, Maggie."

It has been a long time since I was a boy, but time and the hardships of a life in a print shop has not dimmed the memory of the Christmas time when I was a boy. It's sad, but true, I awoke on many a Christmas morning only to find the empty stocking, and I have seen the time when I didn't have the stocking even though Santa might have had the desire to fill it.

The life of a newsboy turned loose on the streets of a city at a tender age is no bed of roses, but if his blood runs red and his heart beats true, he can pick up more fun on the streets than a box of monkeys. And the only reason that I can recall now as to why the trees along our routes weren't full of monkeys, was only because we didn't have any tails.

When I was a boy back in Kentucky the old Yule-tide custom hadn't altogether passed into history. Henry Watterson, one of the greatest newspaper men the country ever produced, was an ardent lover of the newsboys. He mingled with them as much as he did with the politician and the plutocrat, and there was not a newsy on the sheet but would have given his sweet life for Col. Watterson.

On one particular Christmas Col. Watterson induced the business office to put in to practice the old Yule Log, and give the newsies the receipts of their sale while the Yule Log burned. The Yuletide originated away back before the memory of man runneth not to the contrary, and was practiced throughout the south during the slave era. The custom was for the revellers or the slaves to draw the log, always amid shouts and laughter, and not infrequently a rugged and grotesquely marked root of an oak, in triumph from its resting place at the foot of its living brothers of the forest to the wide chimney place. They would then lay the log in the open fire place, soak it in kerosene and as long as the log lasted, there would be singing and dancing and feasting, but when the log burned out all must return to their daily toils.

It's nobody's business just what Col. Watterson told a few of us newsies, but I remember well how Billy Laird, Harry Grinste, and Tude Foster and myself went into the woods, found a huge dead tree, sawed off the "butt cut," bored a big hole in the center, then took that log to the creek, soaked it in the water for ten days, filled the hole we had bored in the center of the log with water and put a peg in the end of the log to hold the water inside, and the business office of the Courier-Journal never was able to figure out why we newsies reaped a harvest for over two weeks while that log was burning.

When I was a boy we celebrated Christmas something similar to the way the boys of today celebrate the Fourth of July. The Christmas season started with us at noon the day before and lasted as long as our money held out, or our credit was good. We shot fire crackers, Roman candles and sky rockets, and the different things we could do with this artillery to aggravate some simple soul, the more fun we got out of it. Tie a box of fire crackers to a dog's tail and turn him loose in a general store crowded with female shoppers, and there is more fun abroad for the next 30 minutes than you can shake a stick at.

And then we kids used to "divide up" and have a Roman candle war, and it was great provided only the other fellow got hit. But say, were you ever hit by one of those burning babies? On account of age, flat feet and 14 dependents, the draft passed me by, but memory and imagination tell me that it is something like shell shock in the late war, and equally as disastrous. I remember one occasion distinctly, and should I happen to forget there is a scar on the back of that knot the good Lord put on top of my spinal column to keep the back-bone from ravelling out, that calls the occasion to mind.

In those good old days I was as much of a Beau Brummel as I am cake eater today, and proud of it—the swellest thing that walks the street. I never got to the point where I cultivated the "light fuzz on my upper lip," but I was a celluloid collar fiend. I wore the highest celluloid neck bands the market afforded, and to my way of thinking I was a Sheik in all his glory. Well, a celluloid collar in a Roman candle war is as dangerous as a chamber maid kindling the fire with kerosene, wherein she takes all your earthly possessions along with her to glory. On that particular Christmas, and in that particular Roman candle war some son-of-a-seacook slipped up from the rear and let drive with a high powered candle, and he got me in the back of the head; the ball burst and the sparks fell on that celluloid collar, and for a week after I had a heart as full of murder as Sing Sing and a conscience that a lady bug wouldn't trip over. I ain't easily bluffed but forever thereafter I had a darn good notion that Roman war candle wasn't a safe game to play, for any way you take it a high powered Roman candle is nothing for a baby to play with.

In later life when I remember how I merged from that war, my neck and face burned to a crisp, my hair singed and my nerves wrecked, and listened to the shouts and hoots of the more fortunate fighters, I couldn't help but think that I was not raised in this age of silk, commonly known as the soft age, for a fellow, though tattered and torn, got about as much sympathy from those chipmunks as a coyote complaining of his woes to an indifferent world.

But the most pleasant remembrance I have of the Christmas season when I was a boy, was sitting around my mother's knee as she told us children the folk lore tales handed down from her mother when she was a girl, and the tales we loved so well to hear.

Mother laid by her knitting and was watching us kids at play when we "jumped her" for a story. So she said she'd tell us one her mother told her when she was a little girl, about a lad and lassie from old Erin, "Twas of a rebellion when the Irish almost broke from the yoke of oppression of the British, but traitors in the ranks, for hope of worldly gain, gave way the plot, and of course, the Irish lost. Then it was that the king's men, with loud and exultant cries rode furious to capture the men of the rebellion, and in each public place hung many a bigget.

The laddie this story is about had led the Irish forces and his name was on the death list with a heavy price on his head.

"There seemed to be no way for him to escape the gibbet, but at last they carried him on an old brig, concealed in a chest. The old brig had been pronounced unsafe for the sea, and had failed to get her clearance, but at the holy hour of midnight, when ghosts and goblins desert their graves, the officers defied all laws, and she sailed away. Then they opened the chest and the rebel so hard sought by the king's men stepped outside.

"The third day out, just as it was getting light a British man-o-war hove insight, and the captain of the old brig cursed and turned a little pale, but he, with the other passengers hurriedly furled the rebel laddie close in the sail, and they didn't find any rebels on that old brig when the king's men came aboard and searched her throughout. And it was well for the rebel that he stayed close and snug in that sail, for had they found him they would have hung him to the yard-arm before he could have said his prayers.

"For 10 long weeks that old brig floundered on the ocean and not a soul aboard ever expected to see land again. Everyone was put on an allowance of a gill of water and one sea-biscuit daily, so that the food and water would last as long as possible. Things went well on this ration for a time, and then all the bread and water gave out, and hope beat low in the breast of every man and maiden on that old ship.

"But one day in December, as the sun was sinking low in the west, the big ball of red burning out the last hopes that beat in the breast of the crew and passengers of that brig, something distant seemed to glitter in the sunset. All rushed to the deck, passengers and crew alike, and the captain fairly shouted as he pulled the last bottle cork: 'As sure as hell was made for the British, yonder is old New York.'

"Next day the old wreck of a ship rounded to 'longside the friendly piers, and people from that ship and from old New York met that hadn't met for many years. It seemed a general jubilee and everything in the old town looked gay. It was all so strange to us who had escaped on the old brig, but we rejoiced that we had been saved the clutches of the king's men, and a watery grave at sea.

"For a time we imagined we had got lost and turned around in the old brig, landed back home, and that it was the king and the king's men celebrating our defeat, and making preparations to hang the rebel we had concealed in the old chest and hid in the sail of the old brig. But as we climbed down the gang plank, and many whose relatives and friends had come on before, met and greeted them with rousing cheers, we learned that we were among friends, and that it was Christmas day."

Father's pipe had gone out and he sat nodding in his chair by the fireplace, as mother brushed a tear from her eye, and closed the story.

"Now children, you may wonder how I remember this story so well, she said, and a deep, sad look crept into her eyes, but children, your grandma was the lassie, and your grandpa was the lad."

It has been many years since my mother told us children this story, and many more since my grandmother told it to her. My mother's once raven hair has turned to gray. As with the good wife we tucked our children to bed, I noticed streaks appearing in my own, and these are the thoughts that ran through my mind:

> "When the embers burn low on the hearthstone of fate,
> And the whitening hair speaks the flat 'tis late,
> I'll pray of thy children, though poorest I be,
> Dear Santa in heaven, forget not thou me."

THE BOYS I PLAYED WITH

Members of "Our Gang" Grow Up and Make Successful Men Though a Little Mischievous in Their Early Youth.

"Percy Howells is richer'n me,
He sure is lucky, all right, 'cause he
Has got shin guards an' a football suit
An' a regular college ball to boot,
But when he gets in a football scrim
I carry the ball much father'n him!"

When I was a boy back in Kentucky our gang had a run that took us all over the town, and if there was any mischief that the membership failed to commit it was because it was not in our catalogue. In the little town of Tompkinsville, where I put in my earlier days, there was a drug store nicknamed "Doodle Bug Corner," where we congregated in the evenings and in this old rookery we hatched up every mischief known to the boys of our day, and right royally we generally carried them to success or failure.

This old building has long since been razed and in its stead stands a fine brick structure. It is a busy business hive today and the memory of old "Doodle Bug Corner" is only a memory in the minds of the older inhabitants who at that time predicted our success or failure in life, according to the crimes we committed on his particular person or property.

But it is not this old rookery that I am interested in, or its passing into oblivion, but the boys with whom I played at that time, and their weal or woe. Some have crossed over the Great Divide, some are serving sentences in the penitentiary, while others have grown up into respectable citizens, become prosperous business men, and are a credit to their communities.

Wiley Dallas was a member of our gang for whom dire calamities were predicted by the gray beards of that little town. Wiley corralled all the marbles in sight, he was captain of the ball team, and the driver at playing at giddy-ap, horsie. Later along he squirmed through examinations on thin study, was the treasurer of his class, and got a rake off on the enamel pins and the group photo, and when he was fifteen he was at work. In the stern citadels of trade he did not find it so easy to lead the field by the nose. Here others were older and had their own ideas as well as their own purposes. But the system wormed a hole big enough for Wiley to squirm through and at the age of 25 he was general salesmanager for a big tobacco company, with his salary jumped to $14 per week and a crew of trade accelerators under him. The sudden elevation, even though he had been climbing all the time, was too big and sweet to be calmly and normally digested, and he had not adjusted himself to the importance of an executive in such a large concern. So a young fellow who until then had been passably reasonable, turned over night into an all-fired big business man, and he grew away from our gang and went to the city. The last time I heard of Wiley he was president of a big tobacco company of his own, thus eradicating the predictions of the gray beards of his youth that the boy was bound for the penitentiary or the gallows.

John Speakman was a leader in our gang, and if there was any devilment that escaped John's young brain, and that he failed to lead our gang into, I have no recollection of it. John's chief aim in life was aggravating Judge Counts, one of the finest old men that ever inhabited that or any other little town, but age had crept into his bones, and an annoying kid occasionally got on his nerves. Speakman, with the rest of our gang, would water the fire in the public room of Counts' hotel, steal the combs left by the chambermaid in the case for the guests, smear axle grease between the teeth, and place them back in the case for future use, and other little tricks which have caused our stern parents to pronounce that unwelcome applaudit: "Come out to the wood shed," had we been caught. And like the boys of today, for boyhood ways have changed but little in the past so many years since I was young, we painted the door knobs, soaped the sidewalk, put castor oil in the whisky, for prohibition in that town was not as strict at that time as it is in some towns today, and other little tricks of a kind too numerous to mention.

It was generally conceded by older heads, that John Speakman, as well as the rest of our gang, would come to no good end when he grew to manhood. But to the surprise of the gray beards his youth ended in a wild, reckless nature that endears itself to the common citizen by its daredevil disregard for the conventions that bind most of us to the prosaic routines of life, and the last I heard of John Speakman he was in the legislature, "but I didn't hear what for."

Abe Vandover always stood at the foot of the class, but sometimes he had a sly way of climbing up. When the teacher wasn't looking he would take his place up the line some four or five heads from the foot, and bulldoze the smaller boys into keeping still. Or if this failed and a word happened to be misspelled along down the line until it reached him, he was always unable to spell it, but would substitute another word, and very innocent like spell out "paper," and walk up to where the word started. He did many other foolish things in school which made the teacher sigh and his mother weep, and caused a meeting of the school board on many occasions to settle his differences. One old-like teacher where Abe attended school was as deaf as a post in his left ear, and Abe had a happy faculty of approaching this teacher with his finger pointing to a word in the spelling book as if asking the pronunciation, then blurting out so that it was audible all over the school room: "You are a terrible old fool, aren't you." But like the Prince of Wales, Abe come from a good family, even though he didn't have much of an aptitude for book learning, and somehow the fates always dealt him a hand that pulled him through. Old gray beards shook their heads and predicted dire calamities for Abe, but he lacked the intelligence to realize his ignorance, and he was always dreaming of better days to come. As he grew to manhood he got a job on the police force, and as every one knows servants of the public are poorly paid, and by sort of general consent, are expected to pick up what graft they can get away with. Well, Abe had the knack, even though his spelling was bad, and he worked both ends from the middle until his accumulations gained to the extent of a clothing store, and now, grown gray with years, his sons and sons-in-law have taken over the business, and old Abe, in his retirement, takes his grandchildren on his knee and tells them that no life is flawless, that no wish is ever wholly realized, that no happiness is utterly complete, that nothing in the world is perfect, not even their grandfather's spelling.

Fred Maxey would bet a four-pound trout to a second-hand minnow on any proposition that came up. He was a gambler of the old school and was proud of it. By the time he was at the young man stage he had more history behind him than Boston, and the same kind of future as one of the linoleum barracks where they put the corpses in pigeon holes. He made his money easy and spent it the same way. He would feed every stray dog or every hungry kid that came along when he was flush, then beg, borrow or steal when he was broke, and life, as a general rule seemed all the same to Fred. He once told me that when he came to the end of the road, if he could "realize and know that during his natural life when little Johnny Jones was terribly hungry he had always given him enough money to buy a chunk of bread, and if he happened to think kindly of him when remembering how he crammed it down, I reckon I'll enjoy it some, no matter whether I'm in heaven or hell." Fred married the banker's daughter of that little town. The old man was high up in financial circles, and his family numbered with the four hundred, and he intimated in strong terms that she was not the daughter her father had hoped she would be. The terrors of a father-in-law didn't worry Fred a bit. He came west "to grow up with the other green things." Being a gambler he joined the oil fraternity, gambling for the bigger stakes. He drilled his quota of dry holes, but he held his head high, and the banker's daughter never grumbled when the hungry coyote howled close to the door, and old-time drillers say there have been times when that selfsame coyote stood on the threshold, only waiting for one more dry hole before making his final leap. It was 18 years ago since Fred Maxey married the banker's daughter. Many things can happen in 18 years, and Fred's gambling luck had made him a millionaire from oil. A few years ago Fred's father-in-law's bank failed. The old man's gray hairs were shaking over the brink of ruin. Fred heard of the old man's financial straits, and when the stockholders were holding a meeting one afternoon to wind up the bank's affairs, Fred walked into the meeting, bought all the worthless paper, stabilized the tottering institution and saved the family millions.

Jim Howard was one of our gang, but somehow or other he never seemed to fit in. When we were tying tin cans to the tail of a stray dog, breaking window lights out of the school building during vacation, or stirring up a nest of bumble bees when the procession was passing, Jim always hung back, arguing with himself whether or not it was right. He was just a kind of hanger on in our gang, tolerated because the boys kind of liked him even though he was always the last to reach the swimming hole, and the first to reach home to help mother wash dishes. True we sometimes called him "Pretty Polly," and asked "have you lost your apron string, sister," but Jim did what his mother told him, just the same, and even in our roughest moments we had a sneaking respect for him that was just a little above what we had for the rest of the gang. Like the rest of the boys Jim grew to manhood, but no bank president jobs, or gushing oil wells awaited him. Like the ox, he was just plain, plodding and useful. He took no chances, played the hands that fate dealt him with a smile, got a steady job in the foundry, married the girl of his choice, and has dragged out an existence on a salary just a little above the scale. He never sought public office, never bet his savings on the horse races, or stayed all night in a poker game after he married. When his 10-hour shift ended he went home, spent his spare time with his wife and a brace of boys, and on Saturday night paid the family budget, and laid a little aside in a savings account. Jim Howard is getting old now. Streaks of gray are showing in his hair, but he still gets in his 10 hours a day, his savings throughout the years have run up to several thousand dollars, a sufficient amount to keep him and his good wife the remainder of their days when he gets too old to work, and this is about all you can say for Jim Howard so far as worldly affairs are concerned. But when old Jim sits down at his supper table, frugal though it may be, with his family gathered around him, he knows for a verity who fawns not upon the master, and who esteems the man, and as I write of old Jim Howard and his plodding ways I can't help but think that I'd rather be old Jim

Howard, the beginning of a poor but noble race of people, than to be the tail end of a broken down aristocracy.

"Percy Howells has lots of stuff
I'd like to have and that's no bluff,
His father's rich and his mother's swell,
But my folks suit me mighty well,
And though my outfit of things is slim,
I'd rather be me, myself, than him."

Millions Seen Through the Smoke of a Cob Pipe Help to Cheer Humanity Along Life's Rugged Road.

"What's the use of dreaming dreams that never will come true;
What's the use of dreaming fickle fortune now of you—
That you're worth a million there is not a doubt,
But what's the use of dreaming when your pipe goes out."

A man who labored nearly a life time in a vain search for oil, which would make him a millionaire finally happened upon fabulous wealth when he drilled in a gusher down in Oklahoma.

All his life "Dry Hole" Brown, as he was known among the oil fraternity, dreamed of the day when he would strike it rich, then settle down and enjoy the proceeds of his find. He drilled a string of oil tests from Pennsylvania to Kansas, and from Kansas to Oklahoma. All were either dry or only small producers—too small to bring him wealth or more than sufficient money to keep his head above the red ink in his bank account. But he dreamed of oil flowing from a gushing well—his own well—at the rate of 10,000 barrels a day, and piling up his bank account. He was of the old school, of the men who believed in pluck instead of luck, in fighting the game square, and in the end the man who played the game from an honest angle would win. As he dreamed he worked, and he argued that no man can pursue a worthy object, with all the powers of his mind, and yet make a failure. "A man may work in the dark," he once told me, "yet one day light shall arise upon his labors; and though he may never, with his own lips, declare the victory complete, some day others will behold in his lifework traces of a great and thinking mind. Men are seen going across lots to fortune; and a poor business many of them make of it. Oftentimes they lose their way; and when they do not, they find so many hills and valleys, so many swells and depressions, so many risings and fallings, so many ups and downs, that though by an air-line the distance might be shorter, in reality the distance is greater than the lawful route; and when they come back they are ragged and poor and mean. There is a great deal of going across lots to make a beggar of a man's self in this world. Whereas the old-fashioned homely law that the man who was to establish himself in life must take time to lay the foundation of reality, and gradually and steadily build thereon, holds good yet."

"Dry Hole" Brown, who dreamed for 50 years of opening a big oil pool down in Oklahoma, and making a million, died a few days before his well came in, and without his dream coming true, but all his life he had the consolation of dreaming of his future, and methinks it was some consolation to the old man.

Jim Bledsoe was known to all the old timers in Wichita. Jim was not his name, but his memory lingers just the same. Jim came to Wichita 20 years ago and started picking up old iron. He dreamed of the day when he would own a big iron foundry in the heart of the manufacturing district of the city. Jim drove a spotted, one-eyed horse to a buckboard and wandered through the back lots and the dump piles, scraping together the scraps the other fellow threw away. He leased a dumping ground on the railroad tracks, and when he scraped together a car load of the old irons, shipped them back east, and received a nice little check for his pains. Old Jim was saving, industrious and frugal. He made more than it required to satisfy his daily wants, and this surplus he deposited in a savings account. He would tell his friends of his profits, his expenses, and the amount of the check he was able to store away to eventually go into his big foundry. His dream was a brick building, a hundred and fifty feet each way, with all the latest and best tools for his workmen to use. Each year, during the twenty or more that he drove the back lots and junk piles of Wichita, he added a little more to his bank account—to the final fullfillment of his dream. Men on the streets would speak in whispers as to what old Jim was worth, when he drove past, and speculate on the day when he would build his foundry, but the dream of a big foundry never came true. He died a short time ago. An executor was appointed to wind up his estate. And what do you reckon he found old Jim to be worth?

He wasn't worth a darn—when he died he was still picking up old iron, and dreaming his dream that never came true.

Charley Clawson owned a 40-acre oil lease offsetting the acreage on which the big Trapshooter well in Butler county, which was the sensation of the oil world some ten or twelve years ago, came in producing at around 20,000 barrels of oil daily. It was the first oil lease Clawson had ever owned, but he had heard a great deal about the fabulous wealth that is made out of oil. He knew nothing about oil, but he was told that his lease was worth a million dollars, and he dreamed of a fine home, race horses, game chickens, Collie dogs, and servants to do his bidding. The big Trapshooter well was gushing oil all over the country, filling the tanks faster than the pipelines and tank cars could carry it away, and men interested in the big well were rated among the millionaire class within less than a week after the oil started spouting out of the ground. The more Charley talked to oil men the faster his dream grew. One of the large companies that had failed to get "protection" near the gusher offered him a half million for his lease, but his dream was a million. Oil men told him he would get it easy. Clawson sent to Oklahoma for a friend—an experienced oil man, one of the heads of the large companies. The oil man came out to the lease, watched the Trapshooter well for half a day, gathered together his instruments of a geological nature and went over the grounds. He advised Clawson not to sell for half a million, or any other price, to make a deal with his company on a drilling basis of one-eighth royalty. Should a well on Clawson's lease come in as good as the Trapshooter well, it would make him several million dollars. Clawson listened to the song of the Siren, was tempted and fell. He turned down the half million offer, dreamed of several millions, leased to the company on a drilling contract, and got a half dozen dry holes, but never a dollar in royalty. Today Charley Clawson is living in a rented house and selling automobiles on commissions. His dream of millions, with a big home and servants and dogs and horses has never yet come true, but he had a lot of fun for a few months thinking he had kidded life out of the secret of success.

Sam Swope, one of the oldest tool dressers working in the Kansas oil fields, at one time dreamed of a fortune from a single oil deal, but he let it slip through his hands. Sam had a block of acreage formed that was worth a half million dollars, and he was offered this amount in cold cash under certain conditions. According to Sam's way of thinking the conditions could be easily met, for his geologists had already made a glowing report on the acreage. Sam had the block completed and the titles in the bank. He had two of the best geologists in the country go over the acreage and geologize the land from every angle. They spent considerable time looking for rocks, alligator bones, dips east and west and other technical points familiar to the rock hounds. They found a good structure with traces of oil, which is unusual for geologists to find. The block was easily worth half a million dollars, and one of the big companies made him such an offer. Sam's pipe puffed free, his belly was full, and the world could go to the devil—"he was setting pretty for life," and his dream of wealth was almost fulfilled. But gold begets greed, and before the transaction was completed another company came along and offered Sam a half million in gold and another half million in oil provided their geologists passed favorably on the land. Sam's geologists had already passed on it and pronounced it good, and he dreamed of two half million dollars, and backed out on his first contract, The company geologists spent some time going over the land. They geoligized it and they core drilled it, and reported "no trace of oil and no structure." The second company was not bound, and they backed out on the deal. The first company didn't want it after that, and Sam let it go back to the farmers and lost his expenses in blocking. Two years later a wildcatter who drills by guess and by God wandered over the country, blocked the acreage and put down a test. He struck a gusher, made a million out of the deal, and Sam Swope's dream of a million turned to a white mad face at the window of his past.

I once had a dream of wealth and position, but somehow or other it never panned out. I wanted a farm, and shortly after the Cherokee Strip opened I went down into Woodward county and started in to prove up a claim. Like most of the fellows who went into the strip in search of homes, I wasn't overburdened with cash, and depended on a job in a country printing office to feed the wife and babies while beating Uncle Sam in the homestead game. I picked a pretty stretch of land some eight or ten miles out of Woodward, and dreamed of sleek calves frolicing over the pasture with tails aloft, of thoroughbred horses grazing in pastures green and Holstein milk cows waddling across the new mown hay field to the milk gap.

I got a job in the printing office at a fairly good salary for that time. I built a little house on the claim that would shelter my little brood, and the blue of the sky underneath floating clouds looked like gold. I hadn't had much experience with work horses, but bought a team I thought was a "humdinger." I hired a nestor to plow the ground and seed the field, and the young corn and kaffir and milo maize sprung up like mushrooms in a manure patch. Life to me at that time seemed great and grand and glorious. The rains had descended, the crops were growing. The horses were fat, and the old brindle heifer was giving a small amount of milk. I was holding down a job in a little town, and the salary was meeting all expenses—but it took it all. Then somehow or other, a paper in an adjoining town began to get all the homestead notices—the only source of revenue for a country newspaper at that time, and the weekly stipend fell off for lack of funds. Troubles never come singly, and in order to keep up the series, one of the horses broke into the corn box and foundered. The old cow broke into the corn field, swelled up and died, and I took the wife and children by the hand and walked off that homestead like a jack rabbit racing a gray hound, for my dream of a homestead had in a year dealt me more grief than every hamburger stand in Wichita could have dealt me during my natural life. But the next year I found that the lonely rocky canyons, the dry naked grass, the wail of a coyote in the early morning, were far more friendly than the streets of a city to a penniless tramp.

It is related that General Sherman once stopped at a country home where a tin basin and roller towel sufficed for the family's ablutions. For two mornings the small boy of the household watched in silence the visitor's toilet, and dreamed of what the big man might be doing. When on the third day the tooth-brush, nail file, whisk broom, etc., had been duly used, he asked: "Say, mister, are you always that much trouble to yourself?"

The boy was Silas Wells, now one of the biggest cattle shippers to the Wichita market, and as he watched General Sherman, he related a few days ago, he was dreaming of the days to come when he could have those same tools with some little fellow like himself watching him perform—which reminds me that

"I am sick of the showy seeming
   Of a life that is half a lie;
Of the faces lined with scheming
   In the throng that hurries by
From the sleepless thoughts' endeavor,
   I would go where the children play,
For a dreamer lives forever,
   And a toiler dies in a day."

IT'S ALL IN THE DAY'S GRIND

Newspaper Man Runs Into Many Things of Various Kinds and Character While Making His Daily Rounds in Search of News.

"All over this nation for years I have wandered,
And many bright birds in my travels I've met,
Recalling the moments and money we squandered
With never a trace of remorse or regret.
I've mingled with singers and actors and writers,
With stars of the diamond since Matty began,
With wrestlers and painters and brokers and fighters—
It's all in the life of a newspaper man."

A newspaper reporter drifting over the city, finds many things pleasant and unpleasant, serious and funny—it's all in the day's grind.

He comes in contact with the rich and the poor, the honest and the dishonest, the preacher and the politician, the Salvation Army lassie and the soiled dove of the underworld. Life is just one conglomeration after another, and the reporter sees and knows it all. In the morning he is in the home of the bank president where luxury is in extravagance. In the afternoon he sees the weeping mother praying for bread for her offspring. On Sunday he hears the most eloquent minister in the city. During the week he sees the poor, degraded drunkard and dope fiend suffering the hell-horrors of delirium tremens—it's all in the day's grind.

In his early days of reporting, he decides that life is "one grand, sweet song." In middle life it all becomes indifferent to him. Extravagance on the one hand and suffering on the other, all jumbled together in his work, crusts his heart, hardens his soul and kills all the finer instincts in him. In later life he sees the pitiful side of the situation, and the heart-hunger and longing, the suffering and sadness appeal to his better nature. But he has long since learned that wealth on one hand and poverty on the other is as "sure as death and taxes"—it's all in the day's grind.

We of the traveling journalistic mold pick up many things during the day, some appeal to us, some appeal to the readers, the paper must be filled, and each day the reporter tries to find something that will endear him to the heart of the managing editor, a soulless machine that is found along with the rest in the newspaper stalls—for it's all in the day's grind.

In the cold, barren hallway of a dilapidated two-story building which nestles below the viaduct, I found Nellie Cameron and her two children, the mother fighting a desperate battle to beat the wolf from the door and keep her children with her, and she told me this story:

During the summer of 1919 she and Charley Cameron were married. They lived in a modest little cottage near the plant where her husband worked. He was a skilled mechanic, and there was always plenty of money for the needs of the family. "I don't know what happened," she said. "I guess he just tired of supporting us and the responsibility of a family. Anyway he left, and two years later when I heard from him he had been arrested and sent to the penitentiary at Lansing. In the meantime I had been working, and managed to care for my two children and keep them together. But the struggle grew harder all the time. Finally I went before the state parole board and plead for a parole for him, and it was finally granted.

"Charley begged me to forgive him, and promised that he would never again leave his children. He soon got another job. Things went well and my youngest child was born. But suddenly, in October, he quit his job and told me he was going to the country to shuck corn. I have never seen him since. Just a little while after Charley left us I was penniless. It was hard work for me to find a job, and often the three of us had hardly enough food for one person. I take the children to the day nursery in the morning and go after them at night. It is a hard life, but I have my children with me, and they are together. We don't have much to eat and wear but the children know that they are getting the best that I can give them." As she finished her story me thought that the Angel of Mercy dropped a tear to blot out the story of a husband who deserted his family. Then: "I asked of a sage who has studied the world from the rind to the core; does love flit out through the window, when poverty knocks at the door?" "It does—on the wings of a swallow, and sometimes I've noticed of late, that love flits out through the window when poverty rattles the gate."

Henry Ford invented the only thing that works without rest and without much need for brains on the part of the person in control. But even a Ford sometimes goes wrong when the nut at the wheel slips. Charley Sanderson was the owner of a Ford and a quarrelsome wife, as many another fellow is today. He was a driver of the kind that has many times failed to harken to the safety first sign at the railroad crossing. Charley had got by for a number of years, and figured that luck was on his side. Then he attempted to beat a freight train across the track at "Dead

Man's Crossing," and they tied. It fell to my lot to report the case and I got there in time to help carry Charley into a house on the side of the road, and all that loving hands could do was done while waiting for the ambulance. For half an hour he lay unconscious, while his wife ministered to him as best she could in his unconscious condition. When he awoke from his stupor the place was deadly silent save for the chirp of a thrush up the hill a distance. It was nearing dusk, the hour when the querulous jay and the barking squirrel quieted down for the night. A screech owl somewhere along the trees took up its uncanny call weird and lonely; and the clear whistle of the whip-poor-will echoed faintly from far down the track.

"Where am I?" Charley inquired, waking from the delirium of fever and feeling the comfort that loving hands had supplied. "Where am I—in heaven?"

"No, dear," cooed his wife; "I am still with you."

The old farmer laughed, but to the reporter it meant nothing, it's all in the day's grind.

Duty sits at the head of the preacher's table. Sometimes the atmosphere of the parsonage is rather solemn; but this is less true than most people imagine. Preachers have usually a well developed sense of humor! I never have forgotten how the jokes and stories flew when the old deacons one day met at our house. But underneath the laughter there is in the preacher's household a vigorous sense that life is a trust, that time is golden, that there is work of importance to be done. This high conviction has not always been a beneficial force in the world. Carried to extremes it has made itself responsible for much persecution and war. But, tempered with humor and tolerance, it has produced the finest characters. Preachers live without fear, in the exalted conviction that the Lord cares for and will provide. They go forward as men who know they are going and have a proper sense of their importance. They do not doubt that the struggle of life is a struggle and not a sham battle, and that the end will prove it to have been worth while.

But the preacher, like most other human beings, sometimes gets in a corner where the circumstances are against him—and I'm not talking about Aimee, either.

The parson had been accused of making love to a female member of his congregation, and the talk was spreading. An old deacon saw him coming from the lady's home one day, and broached the subject to him.

"You misjudge me in saying that I was making love to the young lady, just because we were sitting on the back porch together," said the younger sky pilot. "All right. I believe you," said the old deacon. "Now brush that blonde hair off your shoulder and we'll go on home together." I wrote the story and it never got past the managing editor's desk—but it was a part of the day's grind.

In one section of the city there are no high reaching spires to draw the rich and the great into the fold of Christ. There is a little church around the corner where old women and a few of the older men meet on Sunday nights and listen to the tale of the "Burning Bush" and the "Garden of Gethsemane," but many of the younger generation spend Sunday evening around the depot, in box cars along the tracks, or in the back end of the pool halls.

The Magdalenes walk the street in shame and sorrow, feeling deep down in their hearts the disgrace which they can never outlive. She has been told how the Scripture says that God sees the sparrow fall, but she isn't familiar with any verse relating how He reaches out to catch it before it hits—at least she was not until a short time ago.

It is all right for the preacher in the little church to tell these Magdalenes to go and sin no more, but the trouble is so few of them take the tip. I have often wondered if it were not because anent they did not know where to go.

But there recently came into this a little band of the Salvation Army. Every night, winter and summer this band of faithful men and women may be found on the street corner telling the story of the gospel. It is the hour of worship for the man or woman of the street. It is the only religious service many of them know. Sallow-faced men and painted women shuffle silently into the widening circle, or lurk in the shadows in the background. Forgotten for the moment is the degradation of sinful lives, as one by one members of the little group of workers tell the story of a saving Christ.

The message comes home to many. Some pull their hats roughly from their heads bowed in prayer. Others search silently for coins for the collection. The service closes with an invitation to attend another service at the headquarters. Some heed the call and follow the little band. Those who linger behind to saunter away—who knows how deeply each of them has been touched by the gospel message? Perhaps another night they may remain to be counted with the converts. The newspaper man don't wait to see—it's all in the day's grind.

An aged couple appeared at the Salvation Army citadel and were provided with food enough to keep the wolf from the door for several days. The man was 75 and the wife but a few years the junior. The couple had appeared to return a basket which they had received from the Army for a special Sunday dinner. Not a word did the aged couple utter, which indicated to the lassie in charge that they were in destitute circumstances. The intuition of the commandant at the Army told him to inquire about the larder at the home of the aged couple. "If you ever get hungry just come back," he said as he followed the couple down stairs from the office. Neither answered until they reached the street.

"We're hungry now," the woman finally sobbed, and was saved only from falling to the sidewalk by the supporting hand of the Salvationist. The commandant took them back into the office where a pathetic story of privation was unfolded. The aged couple own their own small home but obstacles climaxed by the old man's failure to find work, has made them destitute. To the Salvation Army head the honesty of the old couple was proven by the return of the basket, and their pride was demonstrated by their reluctance to accept aid, although they were in a starving condition.

The Army again has cheated the Grim Reaper—for a time at least. And it happens with the Army many times during the year, it's all in the day's grind.

Jack Jackson, who operates a barber shop over on William street has as a regular patient one oil man by the name of Jake Hawes. Jake says that when Jack shaves him he uses his ear for a soap mug to mix the lather, and Jack says that Jake's ears are so big there is no other place to put the lather. The conversation, which is continuous, runs about like this from the time Jake enters the shop until he leaves, and still Jake claims he don't pay for conversation. The other day Jake climbed in the chair and Jack put a hot towel on his face that almost scalded him alive. When Jake "cussed" and asked him why he put such a hot towel on his face Jack explained that it was too hot to hold in his bare hands." But what either of them says or does makes little difference to the other, as it's all in the day's grind.

"I once dreamed of being a Byron or Wordsworth,
  I once thought my Muse might sail up to the clouds,
But since Fate won't shove me to heights far above me
  I'm finding my joy in the hurrying crowds,
I'm writing of life and the strife and the scheming
  That sweep me along while I round out my span;
And if this be less than the dream I was dreaming,
  It's all the life of a newspaper man."

WHEN I WENT ON THE TRAMP

Roaming Around Over the Country Is Not What It Is Pictured in the Mind of the Fellow Who Happens Not to Know.

"Once I knew a tramp, the people called a scamp,
And they set the dogs on him else he might steal,
But when he turned away I saw him kneel and pray,
And I know that God above heard his appeal."

While standing on the street corner a few nights ago a stranger invaded my quietitude and broke the silence with the request of the price of a sandwich. I surveyed the speaker carefully, not because the request was unusual, but because the man had not yet attained the beggar's whine and his request carried me back to the days when I was on the road.

I steered him against a lunch counter and watched him chisel desolation into a silver dollar while I listened to his story. Thrown out of employment by the business depression he had started out in the world seeking work, but had failed to find it, until at last he was penniless and hungry in the streets of a strange city. But this tramp has little to do with my story, more than the fact that it called to mind the days when I was on the road, and some of the incidents I witnessed.

Tramps always go in pairs, and when I decided to see some of the world at a small expense, I selected Jim Wellington as my side partner to pilot me around the world on a railroad pass supplied by ourselves.

Starting at Louisville, aside from a racket with a grouchy brakeman and a few questions from the bluecoats along the line, we landed in Chattanooga, a dirty, greasy, sorry lot, but fully up to the standard of the others who were camped in the jungles along the river banks. Early in the morning we invaded the city and landed in the "Hobos Rest," a dirty, dingy, weather beaten saloon where the officers of the law seldom invaded, and squirrel whisky sold at a bargain—a drink and a lunch for a nickel, the lunch consisting of Saratoga chips or a small piece of Limburger cheese which had been cast aside by an up-town dealer.

In this little haunt of hell we got "lit up" and our ingenious attempt to paint the town red did not commend itself as a spectacle to the cops on some of the streets we invaded, and with an eye marked "closed for the season" we were hauled before the squint-eyed gentleman with spectacles, and given 30 days on the rock pile or the privilege of leaving town on the first rattler out, which took us into Memphis.

We loitered around Memphis for a few days, then took the advice of the city officials, mounted the top of a Cottonbelt freight and had a pleasant ride to Texarkana. At this jerk-water station the car icer discovered our location and tender hearted brakeman relieved us of the only two-bit piece that remained in our possession, but with this and liberal use of the hobo balm Jim induced him to give us free transportation to Texarkana, a town at that time divided by prohibition and the slush gang, the dividing line running through the main street of the city.

We of course took the slush side, and soon worked a white aproned bartender out of sufficient number of drinks to see life in a different light, and all the world was at our feet until the town became too small for us and we hiked to Marshall, Texas.

Texas is not a favored resort for the tramp, but at the time we landed in Marshall we were not acquainted with the facts, else we would have turned our course in a different direction. A short time after we made ourselves comfortable at the water tank we heard footsteps on the other side and a gruff voice asked our names, occupation and mode of travel over the country. Our explanation was not entirely satisfactory and we again found ourselves in the toils of the law, on a charge of vagrancy—the same as some of the Wichita business men find themselves today—and were given 30 days on the county farm. And I'm here to tell, though it has been over a quarter of a century, memories of that Texas county farm haunt me until this day. At this hostelry we were given a bounteous supper of sorghum molasses (ever eat 'em?) corn pone and sow belly, and we were looking forward to a nice, quiet rest, then a skip for another section of the country. But our thoughts and hopes were blighted when the overseer brought out a small, stout chain, about two feet long, with cuffs on either end and placed them around our ankles. Then we were shown our places of rest, and the chains around our ankles locked to a long chain fastened to our bunks, when we were left alone in our glory to dream sweet dreams of Texas, hell and the county farm. Next morning we were taken to the cotton fields where, during the long summer day, we passed away the time hoeing the weed that was later manufactured into "silk underwear" for the hoipolloi of the land who have never known the life of the tramp.

We served our sentence, a bitter pill, then hoofed it across the country to Longview, a railroad sub-division, where we took passage on the rattler to Dallas. We had just got comfortably stretched out on the floor of the car when he heard the brakey coming down the line, and finding the door of the refrigerator car open, he pushed it shut, locked it, and again Jim and I were prisoners. Jim realized our position and began telling stories—and they were no jokes—of starvation in a freight car, but I was too tired and knew too little about the real condition to give the matter much thought. I soon fell asleep, little caring about our lot. After what appeared to be a night of rest I awoke, but all around was dark, the train was bumping over the rails, and Jim was "cussing" the luck of a tramp and talking about the sorghum molasses and sow belly back on the county farm. After what seemed hours to me the train stopped, and no brakey appeared to open the door and all our efforts at calling for help proved of no avail. How long we stayed in that box car I never knew, but the gnawing hunger soon passed away and despondency took the place of hope, but eventually the car was switched over to Swift and Company's tracks to be loaded with meats, and when the door was opened and the piercing rays of sunlight shot into that car, it was Jim that still had sufficient courage to kick me back to consciousness and to hope. From the best information we could gather around the yards we had been locked in that car for five days, but to me it seemed like five years, and that possibly played a large part in the game that made me ninety-eight years long before my time.

From here we drifted to Pueblo, got jobs and remained for the winter. But the wanderlust was in our veins, and with the shooting of the green grass we hit for Denver, but Denver was not to our liking, as the I. W. W. were walking on the town and there were more tramps than we found it profitable to associate with. In the blackness of the night we mounted the top of a through passenger train, but in our hurry to make sure of getting out of Denver and away from the horde of tramps that infested that city, we had climbed on top of the express car and got a comfortable position before we realized our mistake. At the rate the train was going we knew it meant death to try to change our location, yet the sparks from the engine, especially when the fireman shoveled in more coal, burned our faces and hands to a crisp, and the heat builded up a thirst for water that would make "the morning after" appear like a dark lantern in a dense fog.

Our troubles with the sparks and the heat, however, came to an end when the train stopped at Green Mound to take water, and we were plunged into the horrors of being ditched in a Utah desert, without food, water or compass. From 10 o'clock that morning, when the train crew drove us from our perch on the baggage car, until the second nightfall, we wandered over that desert no nearer to our destination than when we started out in the morning. But along toward the shank of the evening, out on the open desert, we sighted a prairie schooner and made straight for it in the hope of finding friends, water and food.

Again our hopes were blighted, as the travelers had themselves been lost for several days and both their water and provisions were gone. In utter despair the husband and father had mounted a saddle pony and started in quest of water some time during the afternoon, but had failed to return. Parched with thirst, the gnawing pains of hunger tearing at her vitals, with an infant babe nestling at her breast, the mother had found the spring of eternal life and crossed the great desert into the land that flows with milk and honey, and tramps and hunger are never known.

Before making our dash for the train at Denver, Jim had prepared for the worst, being an experienced knight of the road, and stored a half dozen sandwiches and a bottle of water in a bandanna handkerchief and strapped them around his waist with a cord. We found a spoon in the cooking outfit of the travelers, and for the next half hour I held that little motherless babe in my lap and fed her water from the spoon, after which I took the meat from a sandwich and watched the little mite of humanity suck out the substance with an appetite that would have appeared ravenous in a beast. Then the little lady went to sleep on the arm of her dead mother. We kindled a fire out of the loose parts of the wagon box, in the hope of attracting the attention of any passers by on the desert, then started in for the long watch over the corpse until morning. During the night a traveling outfit had seen our camp fire and in the early morning a horseman rode over from the outfit to make our acquaintance and join us in the march across the desert. We told him our story, and men from his train started over the desert to find the missing father. They found him a few hundred yards from the camp. Having failed in his efforts to find water or the way to civilization, knowing death stared his wife and child in the face, possibly that the wife was dead before he left camp, an empty shell in the chamber of his Colt's told how he had gone to rest.

The little babe was a beautiful, fair haired child, and one of the women in the new found caravan claimed her for her own and faithfully promised Jim and me that she would rear her as her own child.

We dug a crude grave in the desert sand, wrapped the husband and wife in the wagon sheet which had been their last roof in life, the women of the new found party sang "Beautiful Isle of Somewhere," and as they had been in life together they were lowered in the grave, and left alone on the lonely desert to await the final resurrection of the dead. We rode into Salt Lake with the new found caravan, landing in the city after a three-day journey, where we left the party and came back to the States.

I have never seen or heard of the baby girl since we left the party at Salt Lake, but you could tell by the nerve she displayed in sucking that sandwich, and the sparkle in her eye, that she had sand in her little craw, and I'll bet today, somewhere out in the wide world she is making some man a good wife and raising a race of boys who will some day be an honor to their country.

With this last experience I tired of the life of a tramp, came to Wichita, settled down and have tried to live the life of a steady citizen. Somewhere out in the cold cruel world Jim is still following the wanderlust, but when the first blue snow of winter begins to whistle through the peach orchards, a tramp appears at my door, and during the long winter nights we talk of the days that are dead, and my children prattle on his knee and listen to his tales of the world, and beg him never to go on the road again; but with the coming of spring the old familiar itch gets in his feet, and during the spring, summer and fall, he beats over the country as happy and contented as the richest man in the land. And I sometimes think that Jim, while only a tramp, is truly a king, that the stars in the vaulted skies, the sighing zephyrs and the winding streams were made especially for him.

"So if you meet a tramp that bears misfortune's stamp,
  If he's worthy of your aid, why, freely give;
Give him a hearty grip, wish him luck upon his trip,
  An remember that the poor tramp has to live."

DREAMING OF MOTHER

Memories of the Old Homestead Cluster About the Dying Year and In Imagination We See the Old Orchard Where the Children Used to Play.

As the old year draws to a close we of the older generation, whose hair is streaked with gray spend a little time in day dreaming, and these dreams usually carry us back to our early childhood home and mother.

On the banks of Old Mill creek, a beautiful stream which winds its rugged way through the hills and dales, forests and valleys, near the little town of Tompkinsville, Ky., a hamlet near the foothills of the Cumberland mountains, stands a huge log house of 10 rooms and all the necessary outbuildings that go with a prosperous, happy and carefree home in that section of the country.

The old homestead, once the scene of many mountain festivities, now shows the ravages of decay. The chimney has fallen from its moorings, the eaves are caved in and the roof lets in the sunshine and the rain. The chinking has slowly fallen away from the pinnings, the fences are down and weeds and bramble grow in thick profusion over the once rich and beautiful garden. Unused and neglected, the old homestead stands on the brow of the hill, echoing back the rippling laughter of the water; a landmark to the ravages of time.

Across the creek some two or three hundred yards from the house is the remnant of a large orchard; the once beautiful trees now dying from neglect of the pruning knife. Caterpillars have taken possession of the branches and woven their webs from bough to bough. Under the trees where in years agone the merry peal of laughter, the happy shouts of children at play, the dear old tales of love which never grow old, whispered by man and maiden in the heydey of their youth, and coarse voices of men as they come from the fields after the day's work, now answers only to the grunt of a stray hog as he crunches the wind fallen fruit, or gives back the echo of the squirrel that has strayed from the forest in search of food.

Across the glade to the south of the old homestead, leading over to the orchard, is the mark of a path now overgrown with weeds, its course almost obliterated, but which in years gone by, before the children grew to manhood and womanhood and established homes for themselves, coursed its way from the kitchen door across to the orchard where the children used to play.

It is a beautiful evening in the fall, the grass is brown and sear and the yellow leaves, kissed by the blighting curse of an early frost, are fluttering to the ground.

In the remnant of the old path, just outside the garden gate, old age and youth are standing together with poetic fitness; the past typified by an elderly lady, gray haired, keen eyed and bent beneath the weight of many long, weary years of suffering, care and pain. Her face still beams with motherly love and her frail form gives evidence of bygone strength, now supported by the strong arm of youth; the youngest child she suffered to bear—her wayward son—a stalwart, broad-shouldered, firm-jawed young man whose easy carriage and well-developed form are eloquent of good health and free outdoor life.

Age and youth—a mother and her boy are standing in the path, each dreaming of the days that are dead.

The old homestead presents but little contrast to the day 50 years ago, when Buck Maxey came to it with Nellie Conklin, his blushing bride, to found a home, save for the ravages of time.

It was a wilderness then, far back from the haunts and undisturbed by man except the little log cabin which Buck and a few of the neighbors had built, and the garden he had cleared before entering his habitation for the march o'er the rugged path of life with his newly-made bride.

But it presented a sad contrast to the days of 20 years ago, Jack Maxey's first memory of his home and mother, when all was hurry, bustle and prosperity, and the mother's word was gospel in the home.

Today mother and son are standing in the path, viewing the wreck of time; the mother, like the old homestead, emblematic of the ravages of the years, the son in the heydey of his youth; and memory brings days of pleasure and days of pain; tears to the eyes of both mother and son, for the old homestead was a sacred milestone along life's pathway to them both.

Buck Maxey was a worker in his day; and when he took his bride to the little one-room log shanty back in the wilderness, he set about to build a home with fields of ripened grain for the mate of his nest and the little birds that might come to them; and he toiled early and late. When the children—five in all—three boys and two girls—came to bless their home, he added more rooms; another and still another and cultivated his fields and garden until the little hut in the wilderness became the most prosperous and famous home in that section of the mountain country.

The wife and mother was queen, not only of her home but of that entire section of the hill country. Arthur, the first born, was his father's pride and his mother's joy. As she carried the child on her hip from pantry to kitchen, from cellar to garret and from the kitchen to the spring under the hill; or went out to the front gate to meet Buck as he came from the fields and greeted him on his way by holding high in her loving arms the child, her song was merry and her heart was light, for she had something to live for—flesh of her own flesh and blood of her own blood mingled with that of the man she loved.

As Arthur grew to manhood, he was tall and fair, delicate features, large blue eyes, dark hair and an irresolute and undecided mouth; languid, listless, slow but steady; for the stout old Maxey blood along with his mother's beauty had descended to him.

Following in the wake of time came Eugene, who in coming years grew into low stature but stout manhood, with a short neck and hard face; but the dark face was full of character and the thin, compressed mouth, the large well-shaped nose, the restless, fiery eye, the broad pale brow above—intellect was plainly written on all.

Lucille and Julia, each in their turn, came also to bless the home, and as the years sped on both grew to lovely womanhood, the pride of the mother's heart and the joy of the proud father.

As Arthur and Eugene and Lucille and Julia grew to manhood and womanhood, little Jack came to keep comfort and happiness in the home, and he, like the other children, grew into a tall, handsome fellow with dark bright eyes and curly hair—dashing Jack Maxey, with whom young ladies fell in love at sight; daring Jack Maxey, gay, easy, mirth loving, hot headed, but one of the curled darlings of nature, a lover of wine when it is red, of the gambling table and other reckless sports—the wayward son—the one black sheep in his father's fold.

This was the family that Buck Maxey and his wife raised on the old homestead, the children that played in the old orchard under the loving eyes of a fond mother, who, on many an afternoon, tired and weary from the work of the day when it was done, wandered over the path to the orchard where the children used to play.

Fifty years is a long time, and many thorns are encountered along the trail of life during the period. It is only on some occasions, more or less important to ourselves, that we pause in the mad stampede of life for a moment and revert to the beginning—to that commencement which seems so small and laborious, and of the existence of which we almost doubt and many times regret, so insignificant is it by comparison, and so slow the development. Like the boy; to his family and friends he passes from youth to manhood over night, but to himself how tardy has been his growth to man's estate.

Fifty years is a long time in the span of life, and in that space of years, Nellie Conklin, wife of Buck Maxey and mother of his children, saw her boys and girls when they came into the world, and was the first to impress the kiss of love on their brows to enfold them in her arms and give them the nourishment of life.

Mother! Oh, what a hallowed name, so entwined around our hearts that they must cease to throb ere we forgot! Nature has set the mother upon such a pinnacle that our infant eyes and arms are first uplifted to it; we cling to it in manhood; we worship it in old age.

She saw her children toddle from babyhood into youth, and, with her ever watchful eye, followed them into the orchard where the children were wont to play. She watched as they played at hide-and-seek among the trees, and followed them as they scampered beside the creek and across the orchard on horses cut from the willow swamp, and chuckled with motherly glee at their delight and enjoyed their merry songs.

Fifty years is a long time in the span of life, and the mother watched these same children during the brief space as they turned from their youth to the shades of boyhood and girlhood; and pride beat high in her motherly bosom as they started across the fields in the morning to the little log school house down the creek; and many an evening, darning by the fireplace in the corner, tired and weary from the day's toil, she sat until far into the night encouraging the children in their studies and planning for the morrow, that they might be warm and clean and tidy as were the other children at school. After their studies were over for the night it was the same dear mother who crept softly to their bedsides, tucked the covers close around her sleeping children and pressed a kiss of affection on their brows ere she, herself, lay down to rest.

Fifty years is a long time over the trail of life, and in these years she saw her children turn from boyhood and girlhood to manhood and womanhood, and her heart beat high with joy and sorrow as, one by one, each in their turn, passed through the country school and left the old homestead for the town to enter college.

The sacrifices she made, the savings she schemed and the hardships she endured will never be known save to herself and to her God, but each in turn came back from college, carrying under their arms a "sheepskin" telling the good mother and the world that he or she was prepared to enter the battles of life and succeed; and the fond mother was amply repaid for her pains.

Fifty years is a long time along the trail of life and each year bears its burden of joy and sorrow and is fraught with love and tears. Mother Maxey saw her sons and daughters each in turn rising in positions of honor and trust in the world, and she saw them lead the girl or the man of their choice to the marriage altar and start out in the world to build homes of their own. The sons and daughters of her youthful strength, for whom she had suffered and toiled and prayed had gone forth to establish homes of their own, not in the wilderness as she had done, in a log cabin by the side of the stream as she had started, but in the fashionable circles of the city. She was proud to say, "he is my son, my rod and my staff and comforter in old age."

She also heard her children's names sung over the countryside as the leading lawyers and doctors and statesmen of the bailiwick. She rejoiced when their first battles with the business world were won, bringing honor and fame to her household and joy to her heart.

The college had not a single attraction for Jack; he preferred the farm, with its easy going life, his cows and pigs and his sports in town with no staying hand of the school master to guide his course or stop his pleasures. He preferred the farm to the glamor and glory of a city career, and he stayed with it.

Jack was the youngest of her brood, and Mother Maxey wanted him, too, to be a great man in the world, like her other boys and the boys her girls had married.

Fifty years is a long span in a single life, and Mother Maxey saw two sons to whom she could point with pride, whose names were a synonym in the community for uprightness, and carried honor and respect wherever they were known. Two daughters reigning in happy and comfortable homes, and bearing children of her blood to honor the community. And Jack, her wayward boy, the one black sheep in the Maxey fold, who preferred to stay on the farm instead of seeking honor and glory in the outside world.

Today mother and son are standing in the path that leads over to the orchard where the children used to play. Buck Maxey, her companion through life, the mate of her youthful strength, and the father of her children, has been laid to rest in the little cemetery above the orchard, and it's now that Mother needs the children that were to be her comfort and her stay in old age. And it's Jack, the one black sheep, the boy of the farm, who has come to her rescue—to pay tribute for her long hours and days and years of toil for her children.

CAKE EATERS AT FIFTY

Thirteenth Day of January Has No Terrors for Kelly and Me and We Don't Drink Buttermilk, But We Drink Just the Same.

"Don't you weep, my honey,
Don't you cry no more,
Manny's gwine to hold her boy.
All the little white trash rolling on the floor,
Mammy's gwine to hold her boy."

Just because I happened to be 50 years old the other day—to be exact, January 13, and because one E. C. Kelly, traveling representative of the Mergenthaler Linotype Company, happened to be the same age on the same day, the Usual and Unusual man on The Eagle tried to poke a little fun at us by telling 60,000 subscribers that we celebrated by drinking buttermilk together.

Now Kelly is a good Irishman, and I have never been accused of being an angel in the flesh, and when this U.

and U. man attempts to kid Eagle readers into the belief that we celebrated by drinking buttermilk, we both have a kick coming. Buttermilk may be all right for old men like the U. and U. man, but nix on it for me and Kelly. To tell you the plain truth Kelly and me, 50 years old on the thirteenth of January are plenty able to take care of ourselves and have nothing to conceal. We did drink together, but we didn't drink buttermilk. To tell you the plain, honest truth, what we actually did was to drink tea and eat cream puffs, and when our next birthday rolls around, and we are 51 on the thirteenth of next January, if fate plays into our hands like it has in the past 50 years, we intend to have fur on the bottom of our pants—for Kelly says, and I heartily agree with him, there is no use being a "cake eater unless you are a devil of a cake eater."

Well, I was born on the thirteenth of January and am proud of it. I don't know how Kelly feels about it, but I have no apologies to make, and no regrets. My old Negro mammy, who played an important part in my young life, used to sing the lullaby with which this story started, to me in the quiet watches of the night, and she imparted a lot of information into my youthful bosom. Among other things she told me that the thirteenth day of January 50 years ago, was a Wednesday—that Wednesday was a day of woe, that the thirteenth was an unlucky number, and that on that fateful morning, just about the time I let out the first warwhoop of life, a black cat jumped through the window and broke a looking-glass, from all of which she predicted dire calamities for me before I reaped a ripe old age. That dear old colored mother meant well, but she didn't know her boy—she failed to realize that my ability to extract pleasure and sustenance from a hard boiled world, armed with no more visible means of support than nerve and wits was really superb. Neither did she know that I was to be raised back in the yards where a kid at a tender age learns that when a fellow shines a tin can you throw a brick back at him, and that this lesson would go a long way in carrying me over the 50 years of rugged road that I had to travel.

That I shall live to be old I know. It is part of the tragedy; but when my eyes are pale with age, the color and gloss have gone from my hair, and my lips are cold, my hands trembling, I shall still glow when I look back over the years and remember than at a half century there was not a gray hair in my head nor a tooth in my mouth, regardless of the fact that I had been in 13 different states, 11 different jails, married 27 years to the same woman, and never had a minute's trouble in my natural life. But it is beginning to look a little like when I come to the harvest season I am not going to have a bounteous crop of things worth while, that my granaries will not mean security for myself and family, and that the seeds I have sown, and the soil I chose may be the coming true of my old Negro mammy's story of the thirteenth day of the months, the black cat and the broken looking-glass.

In these 50 years, however, I have learned a few things, and among the number is that it's queer, the kind of hand fate, or whatever it is, that rides hard on folks' affairs, deals out. There are those now that I call to mind which appear to cavort all through life a-holding nothing less than threes; there's some that get cold-decked complete from the very shuffle and cut, and then there's still some others which get aces and eights dealt to 'em later in the game, after a considerable stretch of smooth going. Down in Oklahoma where I lived a long time, we—all call aces and eights deadman's hand, and I reckon that's what my old Negro mammy thought I had drawn when I put in my appearance on the thirteenth day of January. Either that or it was a misdeal entirely.

But the years rolled on as all years do. Of the old gang who were born on luckier days, my companions are scattered to the ends of the earth. Some have remained on "Doodle Bug Corner." Some live in Riverside Drive and employ the children of those who remained on "Doodle Bug Corner," and others are buried on a hillside northeast of a town in France called Verdun, but I've stayed on and multiplied and replenished the earth, with never a wave of trouble to roll across my peaceful breast.

I have learned another thing, too, and that is that no life is flawless, no wish is ever wholly realized, that no happiness is utterly complete, that nothing in the world is perfect; that it is a duty to rear our children as best we can, gather in what contentment we may out of life, and close our eyes in death with the knowledge that we have done our best, and that's exactly what I intend to do, barring accidents. I have found that the fellow mortal who follows in the wake of a coyote complaining of his woes to an indifferent world, or a fellow raised under the shade of a crab-apple tree, will get no monuments either here or hereafter. "There is a skeleton in every closet, but there is nothing to be gained by opening the door and rattling the bones," is what my old Negro mammy told me on one of those eventful 13th days of January, and all down through the ages I have kept to her teachings, and that's why there are no gray hairs in my head and an ageless heart is in my breast at the age of 50—but I'm not trying to account for the no teeth in my mouth proposition. I have already told enough lies about how it happened to send me to Sing Sing, and like bobbing the hair, it don't bring youth or retard old age.

It may be true that in some respects the 13th day of January played a part in my life's doings, and that a black cat and broken looking-glass had something to do with my financial luck while traveling along the road of life, for I have so far failed to accumulate a vast amount of this world's goods, but I never robbed a widow or stole from orphan children, and this ought to have something to do with the recording angel crediting me with one or two white deeds to blot out some of the other qualities in my make up. I get a lot of consolation out of the belief that for this act, when I am frying "down yonder" Old Nick will make the fire not quite so hot.

True, I have done a lot of other things that a man ought not to do, but I never got caught at it, and what counts against a man in this life is not what he does, but what he gets caught at. This may not be exactly the way to express it, but my old Negro mammy had some definitions that would have done credit to Mr. Webster, and she told me that "a sinner was a stupid person who got found out," and I believe it, 'cause my colored mammy told me so.

The fellow who gets found out, too, is generally the one you find at the age of 50 swarming with the rest of the drone world at dances and dining parties, and he is the white-haired Freddie when it comes to procuring the necessary stimulants for a select party of methyl suicides, and that's the kind of cattle I stay away from. Possibly that accounts for the U. and U. man on The Eagle thinking me and Kelly drank buttermilk in celebrating our 13th day of January birthday.

True, I may have other faults just as bad, but it has made no white hairs in my head, and some people who have not got the most out of life call 50 years a long time. I may hang over the counter in a box-stall restaurant, sip tea, eat cream puffs and tip the auburn-haired waitress a thin dime for her extra attention, but when the shades of evening begin to fall I remember that this same old Negro mammy, trying to head off the hoodoo of the 13th, told me that there is only one face in the lives of men which soothsayers recognize as being potent as the stars of destiny —only one force that can change a man's life so that he will conquer the stars. It is the love of a man for a good woman. I found her a long time ago, and unlike the boys we are raising today, I have kept her out of the divorce courts now for 27 years, and think I ought to stamp around in that land where they don't shovel snow, with a star in my crown as big as my hat, if the divorce courts don't get us in this age of jazz and family changing fashion.

There is another thing that I have learned, and that is no matter on what day you were born, or how young you may be, if you have ceased to smile you have lost out in the game of life, no matter what your bank account may be. True, it is that every child born expects to write a book, make a speech or run for congress. But a good many of them fail, become dispeptics and grow sour on the world, while others fail, don't realize it, and had rather blow their own horns than to listen at Sousa's band. These are the men who grow old before their time. The average man is sure he is worth more than he is getting—the man above the average proves it, but the average is far in the majority. He understands business about as much as a sparrow on a telegraph pole understands Morse, fails to succeed as well as his neighbor and becomes as sour as a baby orphan mothered by a juiceless aunt, and too many times becomes maudlin with sympathy based on alcohol. Then it is that the other fellow learns his old man appears to have imparted nothing to his firstborn save provender and a roof against the elements.

Spilling out the bunch of stuff anent my age and luck of white hairs, and the other fellow's frailties, reminds me of Shanghi Cloyd and his pension. Back in the hills of Kentucky where I was raised pretty much everybody got a pension from the government for fighting his brother, uncle or grandfather in the War of the Rebellion. These pensioners, having suffered the hell horrors of Libby prison, and other conditions which don't go very far in building up strong manhood, performed but little labor, and their children soon learned to follow in the footsteps of the father. Old man Cloyd resented this fact, and after spilling oaths as long and bloody as Sherman's march to the sea regarding the way the pensioners were squandering their pensions, finally woke up to the cold-blooded facts, and rounded out his remarks with the statement:

"While I'm cussing the other fellow, about squandering his pension, I just happen to remember that I haven't done so damn well with my own."

Any way, I was born on January 13, 50 years ago, a black cat jumped through the window and broke a looking-glass on the day I was born, Kelly and me never drank any buttermilk, I've never been the fellow that my mother thinks I am, but Walter Carr, who puts this type in the paper and whom I sometimes accuse of having grown up under a crab-apple tree and been nurtured on the fruit, tells me that

> "Man's born in this world of toil and care,
> He lives a life of sorrow and despair;
> He dies and he goes—he knows not where,
> But if he's all right here, he'll be all right there."

A GAME OF CARDS

In Life's Pack There Are Diamonds to Dazzle and Lure You to Ruin, Hearts to Deceive You, Clubs to Kill You and Spades to Bury You.

Life is but a game of cards and in the deck you find diamonds to dazzle and lure you to ruin, hearts to deceive you, clubs to kill you and spades to bury you, yet it's everybody's game.

Gambling is as widespread as our country. It is practiced from the humblest water craft to the majestic steamship; from the lowest groggery up to the most fashionable hotels and homes that claim respectability; from the hod carrier in his bespatered rags up to the honorable members of congress.

Gambling assumes a variety of forms from the flipping of a coin in the blind tiger for a glass of aquafortis, up to the splendidly furnished faro bank room, where men occasionally are swindled of all their earnings.

In the game every man and woman, boy and girl must shuffle, cut and deal, and the earlier they learn, possibly the better it is. In the game some hold a hand filled with trumps, while others only hold the long, hungry nine. In leading some throw the ace in the hope of catching the other fellow's trick, while some play the deuce, some the 10, but a larger number play the knave. And thus in the game fools become the dupe of rogues, and rogues cheat each other, even to the point where the old bromide of "there is honor among thieves" is but a recollection, and he is wise indeed who plays the game of life to the end and escapes defeat.

When I was a boy the big poker games were played in a gambling room in the back ends of the saloons, where every device known to the tricksters were in operation, while the smaller games were played on sunny hillsides in spring and summer, and in the barn loft or behind the straw stack in winter or rainy weather. The stakes ranged from a five-cent ante to the sky as a limit in the bigger games, but it wasn't as far to the sky in those days as it is at the present time, while in the smaller games five cents on the corner in a round of pitch was a pretty stiff ante, while penny-ante poker was considered a fairly interesting game where as high as 60 cents could be won or lost in a day's sitting. In one of these smaller games which I witnessed, Jerry Conklin and Bill Grimes were among others in the game. Bill caught a hand of four aces, which was mighty hard to beat in the old days. He looked at his hand for a few minutes and inquired: "Who dealt the cards?" When he was informed that Jerry dealt, he tossed his four acres in the discard, face down, and called: "I pass." Which indicated to me that there were crooks in the old days the same as there be at the present time, as my granny told me while rolling in the cradle.

The games of today are different. Money is more plentiful, and the big oil men who have made their millions over night, sometimes play high, wide and handsome. In a game of stud poker played in one of the big hotels a short time ago four oil magnates were playing with the sky as the limit, and it was mighty high to the blue clouds. In the game were E. W. Dnalram, Jim McWarg, George Rellim and Herschel Enyap, all of whom had more money than brains, and a gambling instinct that outrivaled an Indian. The game had been going for several hours, when Herschel Enyap was called from the room, and in order to keep the game going without a break or a riffle, he asked Bill Yelnats to play his hand until he returned.

Now Bill Yelnats is a mighty good poker player, but a hundred or two dollars is his limit, and he gets heart sick, sufficiently so to have to go to the hospital on some occasions when he loses a dinner where there are four or five in the party, and the dinner calls for choice steaks at the Harvey House. Bill tried to get out of playing the game, but the crowd insisted, and as it was somebody else's money he took a chance. The cards were dealt and Bill had a pair of nines up, Dnalram only had a king showing. Rellim had a pair of treys and McWarg had an ace high showing. Yelnats opened the pot for $50, Dnalram raised it $250, and McWarg raised it $6,000. Yelnats didn't fall over dead but he had palpitation of the heart. He explained to the boys that they had got out of his range, far above his social standing in the community in which he lived, and that the game would have to stop until Mr. Enyap returned. McWarg, who had raised the pot $6,000 was indignant to think that any man would sit in a game and hesitate on betting $6,000 just because he was playing some other man's hand and money. He told Yelnats to put in the money or throw down his hand. This wasn't to Yelnats liking, and he argued that his friend was entitled to play his hand and as the entire bunch had asked him to sit in the game he was entitled to that much courtesy. As the argument waxed warm, Enyap walked in the door, noticed the rumpus and inquired the trouble. Yelnats explained, and without looking at the cards Enyap said: "Call the $6,000 bet and raise it to $10,000. Don't ever stand back on a little thing like six thousand dollars when the other fellow is bluffing." And McWarg, without batting an eye, threw his hand into the discard. His hole card had failed to pair, and the only thing he held was his nerve. Enyap caught the third nine, and had a mighty good hand, but he had never seen it until after he made the $10,000 bet. And now Bill Yelnats, who throughout his natural life had thought he was a poker player, wonders if it's true that a fool and his money are soon parted.

The biggest gambling games when I was a boy were usually played on the steamboats plying the waters of the Cumberland river from Nashville, Tenn., to Burnsides, the head of the river. Big corn and cattle raisers made frequent trips down stream to Nashville with their products, and coming back they were "lousy with coin." The gamblers, men who made a living by their wits instead of the sweat of their brow, would make these same trips, many times in the guise of a rich farmer, to fleece the landlords out of their pay check when returning home. Arch Stone and Billy Laird were two gamblers who made fortunes off the steamboat crowd, and they were not always choice in their methods or modes of separating the yokel from his coin. It was the custom of Laird to go to the boat clerk before the boat started up the river, and supply him, free of charge, with decks of playing cards for the trip, promising the honest clerk a per cent of the winnings for his pains. The cards had previously been handled by Stone, marked, suited and sized, so that he could tell them by the back as well as the face, then carefully placed back in the carton and sealed, so that it would take an expert, onto the trick, to discover that the cards had been monkeyed with. When the game was arranged some of the players would buy a new pack of cards from the clerk, and never a drop of suspicion would attach to any crookedness in the deal. As the game would progress Stone would deal winning hands to Laird, and by the time the farmers reached their destination at least a half dozen or more would be fleeced of all the coin they had collected for sales in Nashville.

John Bedford was a river farmer who made regular trips to Nashville, and was as regularly fleeced for a number of years. But having more than ordinary intelligence, John got onto the game, and framed to get even. He took in as a partner one of the best crooked gamblers in Nashville and explained to him Laird and Stone's deal. Then he arranged with the boat clerk, under threats of exposure and the loss of his job, to accept Laird's cards in the customary way, but when Laird was gone to throw his cards in the river and substitute a few dozen decks that he himself would supply. John's partner in crime had marked the cards to his liking, all unbeknownst to Laird and Stone, who were set on a big cleaning on this trip. Bedford and his gambler partner were easily inveigled into the game. Laird went to the clerk and bought a pack of cards, and the game started. Bedford started winning from the first hand. Stone and Laird tried to read the cards, but couldn't make out their markings. High water had got into the boat and smeared their marks, but they never realized that Bedford was the high water, and as the hands were dealt round Bedford continued to win. Laird and Stone lost every dollar, and Bedford took a bill of sale for their livestock, both owning and operating a farm near Nashville. The game continued, and Bedford continued to win.

Laird switched decks until every deck on the boat had been used, but none of his own markings could he read. Bedford won their livestock, and their farms, and set them afoot at the head of the river without money enough to buy a ticket home.

They tried to borrow fare for return, but Bedford refused. They had to walk. The news spread down the river and to all the surrounding towns. It was a great country joke, and for three weeks farmers along the route would watch for Laird and Stone and hiss the dogs on them as they passed. Bedford cashed the two farms, gave the proceeds to the old folks home in Nashville, and a few years later Arch Stone died in the home Bedford had endowed with his winnings. Laird lived to a ripe old age, but it was said that he never again touched a card.

Bob Kirkpatrick and Bully Bland were playing a two-handed game of seven-up for a nickel on the corner. All day Lady Luck had run against Bob. Bob was a good seven-up player and he knew it. Bully was a poor one and Bob knew it. But Bully kept winning. Bob tried all the gamblers' superstitions to break the bad luck streak, but to no avail. Every time he caught what he thought was a good hand Bully caught a better one, and the queen spot seemed the nagging affair to Bob in the game. Bully always held a queen, and it always proved the high card. Finally, when Bob's last nickel was at stake he caught what looked like a perfect winning hand in a two-handed game. He held a jack, trey and nine. He played the trey and Bully covered it with a deuce. He played a nine and Bully covered it with a ten. Then Bully played his queen and caught Bob's jack, and as Bob played the jack on the faithful queen, and rose from the table, he told Bully: "She, damn her, takes the day."

Cards is the national game, and everybody plays them. Some play for pleasure, and some for the sake of gain. The game is fascinating, and once a victim falls, he seldom gives up the sport. He little knows or cares of the pitfalls into which he is trailing, for a penny-ante has been known to break many a good man, but still we play, and

"When hearts are trump, we play for love,
Then pleasure rules the bower,
No thought of sorrow checks our joy
In Pleasure's rosy hour.

When diamonds chance to crown the deck,
'Tis then men play for gold;
Large sums are often lost and won
By gamblers young and old.

When clubs are trumps, lookout for war,
On ocean or on land,
For horrid deeds are often done
When clubs are in the hand.

No matter how much a man may win,
No matter how much he's save,
He'll find at last a spade turns up
To dig for him a grave."

FOR THE LOVE OF A GIRL

War, Wheat and Oil Play Important Part in Jack Maxey's Life, But It Took a Girl to Save the Man.

It was at the depot at Wilmore, Kansas, when the drafted men for the World War were answering Uncle Sam's call for the first quota from Comanche county, that Jack Maxey realized there was a serious aspect to his side of life.

For the other boys who had formed the quota, fathers were there to give them advice and cheer them along toward the front. Mothers and sisters were there who cried and kissed their sons and brothers good-bye, but Jack stood alone, with no one there who cared for him. Deep down in his heart he wondered what he was going to fight for, and why he should go at all.

Jack was left an orphan at a tender age, and had grown up in the village of Wilmore. Since he was ten years old he had been compelled to hustle for himself. In this early period of his life many a night he had crawled into an empty goods box hungry and disgusted with his lot, and sore at the world. As he grew older his condition improved somewhat, but still he was kicked and cuffed about the street so much that he became case hardened and cared little what happened to himself or any one else.

As a boy he was a leader in all sports. When a watermelon patch was raided Jack was in the gang. When a dog went down the street with a can to its tail, Jack could be seen looking around a corner at the alley with a guilty smile on his face.

And thus he grew from boyhood to manhood, with no father to restrain him, and no mother to weep o'er his erring ways. As he stood on the platform waiting for the train to pull in and saw proud fathers speaking words of encouragement to their sons, and mothers and sisters weeping over the departure of the ones they loved, his heart sank, as he realized in all the wide world there was not a human being to grieve over his departure.

Once in his life, but only for a few brief days, Jack had thought he had something to live for, and had braced up to be a man. The vision lasted only a week, and he sank back into the wild, reckless life which had gained him the name of "Dare Devil Jack."

It was the time of wheat harvest when Jack left the streets and went to harvest for Frank Jackson. It was there for a week he lived the life of a real man, with hopes high for the future and a better idea of life in general.

The header broke and all the men except Jack had pulled into the barn waiting for repairs. Jack had remained in the field, alone with his thoughts and his bitterness against the world. He was leaning against the barge outside the ripened grain—perhaps there was a breath of sound, he could never remember, but for some reason he lifted his head just as the waving banners of ripened grain parted and the face of an angel looked through.

Parting the grain was beauty of which he had never dreamed. A sapling of the forest was not straighter nor rounder than her slender form. Her soft waving hair clung about her face with the heat, and curled over her shoulders. She was smiling on him in perfect confidence. The smile thrilled his entire being and awakened in him thoughts he had never dreamed of before, and the wildly leaping heart of Jack Maxey fell in the shattered grain at the feet of Nellie Jackson with such a thud that he did not understand how she could have avoided hearing it—and woman like, she did hear.

As she moved across the stubble toward him he had hard work to keep from falling on his knees, for they were weak, and he was hard driven by an impulse to worship her.

She came to the header barge and talked to him until the men returned, and all during the afternoon he worked harder than he ever worked before. For the rest of the week he dreamed of the evenings when the work would be over and he could go to the house, for after the dishes were done Nellie would come out on the front steps and talk with him for an hour before retiring for the night.

Frank Jackson knew Jack, as every other man in the country knew him, for he was not asleep as to his surroundings. Saturday night he gave Jack his pay check and informed him that his services were no longer needed.

Nellie had been taught above all things to obey her parents, and her father informed her in words so plain that she thoroughly understood, that she must not speak to Jack Maxey again.

It was then that the only hope, the only friend and the only ambition Jack ever had was killed. His old life was tame compared with his return from the harvest, and he sank deeper into the slough of despond.

It was generally conceded that Jack would never amount to anything in this world or in the world to come. The best people shook their heads and wished he was out of the community. All pronounced him worthless and he realized to the fullest extent their thoughts and opinions.

Many times he passed Nellie on the streets, but she never recognized him. He never glanced at her, and three years had obliterated many thoughts of her from his memory.

As he stood on the platform, going forth to fight for his country which held for him no home, no sweetheart and no friends, he felt that every human being in the village was glad that he had been caught in the draft and was going to leave.

He dropped on the edge of the platform with his head between his hands. Never had the terror of loneliness fallen upon him as it did this morning. All the other boys had something to live for, something to fight for, but there was nothing that bound him to a single tie. A strange hatred for the world fell upon him. He had grown accustomed to loneliness, to being unnoticed, but never had he known what it meant to have someone really care for him as the other drafted boys had. He heard the sobs of mothers weeping as the train was heard in the distance, and the sounds came to him as from another world. The muscles of his mouth twitched tremulously and he shivered as if stricken with a cold. He bit his lips and cursed the fates that had sent him to fight for—nothing.

When Nellie Jackson came down to the depot with the other girls to bid farewell to the soldier boys, the first sight that met her gaze was Jack Maxey sitting on the edge of the platform, apart from the crowd, his eyes downcast and his countenance moody. Although she had not spoken to him since the day her father sent him from the farm, she had secretly loved him, and silently wept at his rowdy career. She made up her mind that regardless of what her parents and the whole town might say, when Jack started to board the train she would tell him good-bye, and that she for one would pray for his safe return.

She stood with the other girls at the edge of the crowd, her eyes fastened on Jack's face. She could not take them away. She crossed the platform with rapid step and laid her hand gently upon his arm. Her heart ached at his changed appearance and moody countenance; he seemed so heart hungry, so utterly helpless and so alone. For once she tried putting herself in Jack's place. What would it mean to have no home, no parents, no friends and a disreputable name? A disreputable name—that was the worst of all. She lifted her hands to her dazed head and reeled as Jack looked up and faced her. She dropped on her knees, slipped her arms about his neck, and leaning over him, sat her lips on his forehead.

Jack looked up into her eyes, his face crimson. It cut him to the heart. His form shook, his muscles quivered for a moment, then he noticed the crowd staring at Nellie, and realized the disgrace she had on herself.

She lifted an unashamed face and bravely laid her quivering lips on his. Her breath was like clover blossom in his nostrils and her hair touched his face. Then she looked into his eyes and said:

"Wild as you may be, I hate to see you go; I want you to give up your past and make a reputation as a soldier and come back home a better man."

Jack listened, earnestly, attentively. All the fire of his misspent life burst in his heart. All the misdeeds of the past rose before him, and his nerves went wild. With the crowd on the platform staring, he bent over the only girl he ever loved; the girl he had not dared look at for fear of disgracing her, then caught her in his arms and held her to his breast. Then of a sudden he caught her by the shoulders, held her at arms length, gazed long into her face as if impressing her every feature on his memory, so long that the train whistled, the conductor called "all-aboard," the bell rang, the crowd stared and wondered, and the train started. Still he held her by the shoulders and looked into her eyes. The boys in the coaches called for him to "come on." The train began to get up speed and move away from the platform. Above the din and noise the crowd heard Jack say:

"Good-bye, little girl, 'm fighting for you!"

The train was 50 yards away and going at full speed, but it had no terror for Jack. He raised his hat to Nellie as she held out her hand to bid him farewell, turned and waved at the crowd and started after the train on a run—as wild a race as he ever made on the athletic field or at the county fair.

Whether or not the engineer saw him racing after the train and slowed down the engine, or whether he beat all records and outran the locomotive, the crowd could never tell. They saw him gaining on the train, saw him run alongside the coach, grab the rods and swing on the steps, waive his hat to Nellie and disappear inside the coach.

Old men and women shook their heads at Nellie's actions, while she, scared and ashamed, rushed home to receive the cruelest reprimand that ever fell from the lips of her father. She heard little that he said, for her heart was far away, following Jack Maxey across the prairies to the war.

Had the crowd on the platform noticed more closely as Jack started the race for the train they would have seen a new light in his eyes and a different smile on his face, more seriousness in his countenance, for now he had something to fight for, and he was happy.

Nellie's act at the depot when Jack left was never forgotten. It was discussed in the sewing circles, at church gatherings and in the parlors, and the conversations were many times carried to Nellie by some meddlesome Mattie, but she continued to pray for his safe return.

Jack Maxey found himself mustered out of the service with only a few dollars in his pockets. His first thoughts were to rush back to Wilmore and claim Nellie as his bride, but when he thought of his reputation there, and without a dollar in his pockets he gave up the idea and stopped in Wichita, where he went doggedly about the city in search of a job.

After weeks of search he landed a place with an oil company. The oil game is a gamble, and Jack had always been a good gambler. The syndicate drilled a producing well on its lease and Jack cleared a few hundred dollars in commissions. He purchased a lease with his savings near a drilling test and it came in a producer making his acreage valuable. He interested a drilling company in the deal and a test was started. A second test near his lease came in a duster. Geologists pronounced the territory dry, and the drilling company, at the first sand depth gave up the test. Jack walked the streets like a whipped cur and cursed the luck that brought him from the army.

In desperation his old dare devil spirit returned and he went to work to complete the well. He went to the friends he had made in the oil game, and with many promises and much persuasion raised sufficient money to start the drill going again.

He read in the newspaper that the mortgage on the Jackson homestead was going to be foreclosed, and he wanted to help the old man, but he was broke, penniless and financially ruined as the result of his trying to drill an oil well.

"But the years, we are told, seldom prove unjust." When the last dollar Jack could possibly raise was gone, and even the drillers had given up hope, the bit ran into pay sand and oil shot over the top of the derrick and Jack Maxey was a near millionaire as well as an honorably discharged captain of the World War.

As the crowd gathered around the court house steps in Wilmore to bid on the old Jackson homestead a clean-cut stranger in a big car stopped to the edge of the crowd. The bidding had started and there appeared to be a lively interest in the sale. When the bids had reached the value of the farm and the auctioneer began the "once, twice," in slow syllables, the stranger looked out through the car window and called:

"One thousand dollars more," and the sale ended.

When the auctioneer inquired of Jack the name of the purchaser Jack handed him a certified check for the amount, as he gave the name as "Frank Jackson."

"The same dare-devil, son-of-a-gun," was the sheriff's comment as he stepped to the telephone to notify old man Jackson that he, himself, had bought his farm.

At early candle light in the little town of Wilmore that night Jack Maxey and Nellie Jackson formed a partnership for life, and the crowd that stood on the depot platform the day Jack left for the war learned that love can save a bad man as easily as it can wreck a good one, according to the mysteries of human nature, as be like the peace of God himself, past all understanding.

ECHOES FROM THE STOCK SHOW

A Good Horse Always Shows His Strain Though the Finest Man That Ever Stepped May Have a Son That is a Quitter, Says Deane Gill.

"I love the hoss from hoof to head,
From head to hoof and tail to mane;
I love the hoss as I have said,
From head to hoof and back again.

"I love my God the first of all,
Then Him that perished on the Cross;
And next my wife, and than I fall
Down on my knees and love the hoss."

The big stock show held in Wichita a week ago brings memories of boyhood days, back in old Kentucky, where so large a portion of the population derives its living from the production of thoroughbred horses. But all lovers of fine horses are not confined to Kentucky, as some of the Kansas exhibitors at the livestock show a week ago will bear evidence.

I have heard as how Judge C. C. Stanley, trained as he is in legal battles and the oil royalty game to conceal his emotions, threw himself on a sofa and shook with sobs a few short years ago when he received word that his favorite saddle horse had been injured and would probably have to be killed. And I heard this same Judge Stanley bitterly rebuke a horse trainer for using the whip on another person's horse while getting him ready for the show ring. And I have also heard tell as how this same Judge Stanley once stole away from a party of celebrities and disappeared: they found him sometime later, his arms clasped about the neck of Lila Lee when she won the championship at the stock show. And the only connection Judge Stanley ever has with Kentucky is when he visits the state to buy a thoroughbred horse. An hour's conversation with Judge Stanley about horses convinced me that he is a great lover of them because he is a great man.

A Kentuckian bows the knee only to his God, his sire and the ladies, but I have heard as how Deane Gill of Eureka, bows to Kentucky Spider, the head of his string of thoroughbreds, and Gill is a typical Kansan, who makes his money out of Kansas oil and spends it on Kentucky horses. Mr. Gill will tell you that the nobility of the thoroughbred horse is unquestioned, even by those who have discovered an occasional rogue in the breed, and it has a well nigh universal appeal to the heart of man.

Perhaps it is because men who hold positions of responsibility often yearn for the true and the beautiful that Mr. Gill is happiest when he can repair to his stables and spend a few hours with his horses, and perhaps too, it is because his years in the oil game have taught him that a man can't trust anything that walks on less than four legs, in the game of life. Mr. Gill tells me, too, that a horse always shows his strain, though the finest man that ever stepped may have a son that's a quitter.

The thoroughbred horse always calls to mind the turf. We do not hear so much nowadays, of fiery challenges and caustic acceptances, as when I was a boy, but the lovers of thoroughbred horses love to remember the glowing tales of the turf in all its glory. Bill Lassen, a devoted lover of a thoroughbred horse, tells me that the match race, epitome of sportsmanship, has almost passed from the turf. The proud sportsman who owned he had a good horse, and defied his associates to trot out a better one, now too often courts contempt for his horse for the longer odds that contempt will bring. It is pleasant to think of a racing world, says Mr. Lassen, with more Johnny Harpers in it. It was Uncle Johnny who brought the immortal Longfellow to the turf with an open challenge, an sadly laid him away under the apple tree by his window when his career was ended. A cot in his horse's stall was good enough for him, and no man's wager against his horse went begging while his money lasted. He made his own "book," and warned each and every one that no horse lived greater than Longfellow, while he accepted the money they proffered to bet against him.

"But," said Billy one time after watching his money disappear in Uncle Johnny's satchel, and waiting in vain for a slip, "how will you remember me when I come back after the race?"

"Son," replied Uncle Johnny, "you ain't comin' back."

A horseman will tell you that use of the whip is indispensable to getting the best out of many horses. This is probably true. The human race has no monopoly on indolence, and it is just another evidence of their humanness than many horses need occassionally to be reminded of the task at hand. But also like human beings, Jack Vickers tells me, horses resent prodding when doing their best and are likely to show that resentment with a pointed refusal to try at all. Mr. Vickers will also tell you that scores of potential victories are turned into defeat in this manner. "He went to the whip and tossed the race away," is one of the most common expressions to be heard where racing is talked. You can't throw a good horse off his feed by cutting out one meal, says Mr. Vickers, but you can throw a race or a show with a fool and a whip trying to handle a horse with more sense than its jockey. A horse must be broke before he will work, and it's just so with men, in a good many cases, and I think too much of the horse and his fine human sense to let any trainer use the whip and spoil the horse. Whether in the show ring, on the race track or the polo game, Mr. Vickers requires his riders to go without a whip. When Mr. Vickers boosted a rider on his horse as he entered the ring at the stock show the jockey insisted on having a whip. "Well, if you must," said Jack, and he pulled a whip from the store room, broke off about six inches of the small end and handed it to the rider.

Jack Turner prides himself on having the best horse in the country, and taken by and large it is a pretty good horse. Jack had his horse matched at the stock show with some of the best horses in the country and walked off with his share of the blue ribbons. With one of the other entries there was strong competition, and possibly a little jealousy, and the other entrant was terribly disappointed when Mr. Turner's horse copped the ribbon, as the other party thought his horse unbeatable by a local animal. Social feeling entered into the controversy. The other fellow was aspiring, while Mr. Turner prides himself on being no better than his neighbors. "If you will come to the country club I will match my horse against yours for five thousand dollars on the side and let three of the best horsemen from Kentucky decide between them," said the gentleman of animosity. "If you will come over to my coal yard I will match my horse against yours for ten thousand dollars on the side, and you can pick the judges," replied Mr. Turner.

P. H. Clark from down at Tonkawa, Oklahoma, came to the show with one of the finest strings of horses seen in

Wichita for many a day. Mr. Clark carried back to his oil home a bunch of blue ribbons, and every one of them was won in the closest competition, against the best imported Kentucky horses that money could buy. There were saddlers and trotters and rackers, canterers from California to Texas, and each horse represented the pick of their respective stables. One of the things that Mr. Clark knows about a horse is that the trainer either makes or ruins the horse, and he does it in short order. In order to give his horses every advantage, Mr. Clark, in addition to handling Kentucky horses, has a Kentucky trainer to handle these horses. Just about time one of the entries was ready to enter the show ring one of the show attendants rushed in to Mr. Clark and informed him that he didn't think his rider from Kentucky was in good condition to ride the horse at this particular time and in this particular entry. "Tell him to mount and come on in the ring," directed Mr. Clark. "No man from Kentucky ever got in a condition where he could not ride a horse."

Frank Coddell lives out in the Wilmore country, and in the days when Oklahoma and Kansas were young, Mr. Coddell was a great race horse man. He owned a long, lean, shanky animal that looked like it had never seen Kentucky, but it could outrun a sway-back mule on any race track. Mr. Coddell, after the harvest season was over, took his horse and went around the country, backing him against any horse to be found in a quarter or a half mile race. Mr. Coddell always made Alva, Oklahoma, with his race horse, and invariably "took the boys to a cleanin'," for his horse was a runner. Bill Clifford was always one of Mr. Coddell's victims. Bill had a sway-back mare with a knocked down hip, and Bill actually believed she could win in a walk, but she couldn't. One day Coddell drifted into Alva with his race horse, and no sooner had Bell heard of his arrival than he came to town with his old gray mare, "itching for a race." Coddell's horse had beaten the old mare a half dozen or more times, and beat her as many lengths as he wanted to. It was simply a town joke, but Bill took the matter seriously.

Bill had saved a hundred or so dollars and he bet it all. He pawned his watch and bet the proceeds, he sold another horse, his bridle and saddle for less than they were worth, and bet it all. Everything he could raise money on he parted company with, and bet it on the race. Coddell, thinking Bill had gone crazy, tried to call off the match. It was too much like taking candy away from children. Bill's friends tried to stop him in his mad bets, but to no avail. There was talk of calling the insanity board together and confining Bill where he could butt his head against padded walls. But still he bet—bet it all, all he had, all he could borrow, and all he could beg. And then the race started, and that old gray mare with a knocked down hip went down the track like Nancy Hanks in all her glory. With head and tail up, eyes ablaze and standing out on stems, she left Coddell's horse half a length behind at the first jump. At the quarter stretch Coddell's horse was running three lengths behind, and when the old gray mare came under the wire Coddell's race horse, that had beaten her half a dozen times, was so far behind that it was hard to guess that he was in the running, and it was a year or more before Coddell or the race fans around Alva learned there was such a thing as doping a horse and beating the world.

J. A. Wood, of the Bridgeport Machine Company is one of the greatest horse lovers in Wichita, and owns one of the best horses. Mr. Wood's horse entered the strongest competitions at the big show, and carried off his share of the ribbons. He thinks the Kentucky thoroughbred the best horses. Mr. Wood has owned a number of fine Kentucky animals, and he has been so well pleased with his Kentucky horses that he has come to the conclusion that anything that comes out of Kentucky is good. A short time ago Mr. Wood wanted a young man to train as salesman for his company. Mr. Woods was to find the best young man available, train him to his own ideas of salesmanship and have a man that would be a worth-while young man in the organization. In his effort to find this particular young man Mr. Wood inserted an ad in a number of papers over the country. Shortly afterwards he received a letter from a chap hailing from the blue grass regions, and giving a number of business men as references. Mr. Wood wrote to one of the references and received a letter immediately stating: "The young man comes from a fine ancestry. His forefathers were lords and ladies in England. His great grand ancestors came over on the Mayflower and first settled in Virginia. His great grandfather was one of the pioneers who came into Kentucky with Daniel Boone, and his family tree carries among its branches, governors, senators and legislators of the highest character and types." After carefully studying the letter Mr. Woods replied: "My dear sir, you evidently misunderstand the kind of man I am looking for. I want a young man for a salesman."

In addition to the horse show there were a lot of dogs at the dog show—bulldogs, rat dogs, Collies, Danes, fox hounds, in fact all kinds, and some with the funniest faces I ever saw, and one particular breed of "little big" fellows, they told me was a laughing bulldog, but what the devil he was laughing at I don't know.

ROAMING AROUND

Travel Wasn't So Fast When I Was a Boy, But Life Run Along on the Level and We Got There Just the Same.

Yesterday I walked down the street, quiet and peaceful like, attending to my own business and not bothering anybody. As I started across the street a big copper began to blow the emergency whistle. Thinking he was blowing for assistance of other cops I meandered along across the street. But I didn't get far until the big copper caught me by the arm and dragged me back to the corner, all the while sputtering something about yellow, green and red.

I tried to pilot a friend of mine from Wilmore from The Eagle office down to the depot in time to catch a train. We hit all the crossings at the wrong signal, and got there 45 minutes after the train had pulled out. Disgusted like, my friend looked at the electric contraption in meditative mood for a long time, then told me confidentially: "We don't have no such fool things as that down at Wilmore. And he swore by all the eternal heifers on the farm, that hereafter he would do his walking in Wilmore, where a free, white, respectable citizen can cross the street at any time or place he wants to without having to look yellow, red and green all at the same time.

But with all its faults, the traffic signals are good things, and may possibly save some fool dyspeptic from getting killed, but I can't help but think that like the flies and skeeters, it's the sort of contraption God causes some nut to invent to curse the earth as it rushes headlong in its mad desire to get somewhere before it needs to.

Down in Kentucky where I come from, we had no traffic signals when I was a boy. If a fellow wanted to cross the street he crossed it, and if some old guy with a horse and buggy run over him it was his lookout. That was before the days of a "fool and a Ford," and the fellow who was riding had some respect for the fellow who was walking.

Neither did we have any section lines to travel while going from place to place, as we do out here in Kansas. When we came to the forks of the road there was generally a friendly guidepost to tell us whether to go to the right or the left. But if you stopped at a farm house to inquire the way, as a fellow sometimes does, the farmer wouldn't direct you to go so many miles west, detour to the section line, detour again to the main road, follow the section lines east to your destination.

But the farmer would tell you "go up yonder about three-quarters of a mile until you come to a hollow stump at the side of the road, turn to your left and go two miles straight ahead until you come to a new ground, turn to the right and go down by Jonah Emberton's peach orchard, cut around the peach orchard until you come to the left-hand corner, then turn to your right and follow the main road to the head of the spring branch, turn to your left and keep straight ahead until you pass a forked persimmon tree, and the third house on your left will be the place you are looking for."

We didn't have steel and concrete bridges, either, back in the days when I was a boy. When we had to cross the creek on foot we walked across on a foot log, and when we were horseback or in a wagon or buggy, we forded. Fording the creek was all right when the water was low, but sometimes, in the spring of the year when rains were more plentiful and the creeks were full, it was a good idea to pray before venturing into the ford. I remember one time when I was visiting an uncle down in the country who lived close to the creek. A dapper little drummer in plaid clothes and kid gloves drove up to the house one day and hollered "hello." I went out to the gate, and the gentleman offered me a quarter to go with him down to the creek and show him the ford. He thought I was a farmer boy who lived there, and a farmer boy generally knows all about the creeks near his camping ground.

I climbed into the buggy and rode down to the creek. The gentleman said nothing more about the quarter he was to give me, and I wasn't very much interested in the ford. However, we came to the creek and the water was out of its banks. I suppose there was a ford there when the creek was low, but I never let on that I knew anything about it. I was a smart boy from town, and this particular guy thought I was a wool-hat boy. And, besides, he made no effort to pay me the quarter, and I didn't have sufficient faith in his honesty to believe he would throw it back across the creek after he got over, even though he might be a baseball pitcher with a good arm.

I looked around the creek bank for a few minutes, then said: "Here is where my grandfather always crossed." I didn't, however, tell him that grandfather had been dead these 20 years and the ford might have changed. The dapper little fellow drove in, and the first dash out of the box, horse, buggy and driver went under the water like an otter. The next I saw of the outfit, it was 20 yards down the creek and the rushing current was sending horse, buggy and driver in a mad rush down the stream among floating timber, logs and stray limbs that had been picked up by the flood tide.

A farmer in a nearby field heard the dapper little driver yelling for help and rushed over to the creek bank. With his work team and a rope he finally managed to pull the fellow and his team out on the bank he was trying to ford to, and after patching up his buggy and harness and giving his horse a rest, he went on his way rejoicing. But he stopped at the country store about a mile away and left me my quarter and a 50-cent copy of the New Testament.

We didn't travel as fast when I was a boy as we do today, but if I remember history aright, we traveled a good sight longer. Adam lived 130 years before he had a son, whose name was Seth; after that he lived 930 years; then he died. Cain lived 840 years after he begat Mahalaleel, then, if I read aright old Methusaleh lived 900 years, and this happened even before my time. Instead of the automobile which carries us at the rate of 60 miles an hour, we spent at least two days making this same distance with a horse and buggy, but we had more fun on the road, our nerves were not so highly strung and we got there just the same. The little town in which I was raised was 30 miles from the railroad. When we wanted to see the train we traveled to it on horseback, or in a buggy. It took all day to make the trip. We didn't have paved roads, and sometimes the mud was ankle-deep to the horse, but we jogged along without any traffic cop to stop our speed and insult us on the way. We weren't bothered with hijackers and we burned out no bearings, and death and destruction from a fool in a Ford was not lurking on every turn in the road. Of course, sometimes, a horse hitched to a buggy would run away and tear things all to smithereens, but the fellow passengers on the road always had time to get out of the way and we didn't have to worry about damage suits, or the murder of women and children by our carelessness. Noting the rate of speed at which we now travel, listening to the ambulance siren speeding to an accident half a dozen times a day, and reporting column after column of mangled bodies and broken bones throughout the week, we sometimes think that old Methusaleh with all his strength and knowledge of the art of living, might not have reached his allotted time had he sped down the street necking a blonde gold digger, as some of the promising youth of today are doing on the public streets of the cities.

Having grown up under the old dispensation it is hard for me to get the hang of present-day operation. However, I bought my wife a second-hand Ford to replace the horse and buggy, at twelve o'clock, and she got run over at two. When I climbed in behind the wheel I put one foot on the starter and the other on the brake, and the thing wouldn't run. I changed feet and changed pedals and it went around the corner like the claws of a tomcat through a summer undershirt. I made it fine around the corner, but another fool in a Ford got in the way and his car was sent to the junk shop. When I left the scene of the wreckage I saw a motorcycle cop coming up the street. Some one had telephoned the police station, and he was exceeding the speed limit. So was I. I missed that copper about a quarter of an inch. I was afraid, when I saw him coming, that I was not experienced enough to hit him, and I was right. While I missed the copper I hit a plate-glass window two blocks down the street, and went through the store like a wharf rat through an alley. Then it was that I began to realize that a Ford can slip you more trouble in five minutes than all the hamburger stands in Wichita in a year. The police judge thought I was paying off the wages of corn and he gave me a lot of advice and a $25 fine. The fine wasn't so bad, but I sympathize with any intelligent human being who is forced by law to listen to the advice of a police judge in an agricultural district.

My wife thought I was not capable of driving her car, and in order to get back into her good graces I bought her a new dress, which threw a lot of light on the subject of my ability to drive. When she got that dress on she wanted to go down town to a picture show. I made a nice drive of it to the theater, but arrived five minutes late for the picture. As I neared the show place I set my foot on the brake and slowed down, and the wife, in her hurry to see the start of the picture, dashed through the car door. As she jumped out, the door closed with a bang, and being in a hurry to get to the office. I started the car in high. The tail end of that new dress caught in the door. I heard a tear, and thought I had stripped the gears. That infernal machine kept rushing on, for I had my foot on the wrong pedal to stop her. As I turned the corner I looked back. There stood my wife on the sidewalk in front of the theater. Visions of the picture had departed and so had most of that new dress. I haven't driven an automobile since.

Now, then, I sometimes wonder, if everybody has gone to the hospital when we get to the end of the lane, what's the use of making the journey.

DAYS THAT AIN'T NO MORE

Memories of the Old Saloon and the Boys We Met Around the Flowing Bowl.

Since Mr. Volstead preached the funeral of John Barleycorn there has been a question as to whether or not he was dead. I don't know. But I do know that you can kill a snake in the middle of the day and his tail will wiggle until the sun goes down, and some times I think I see old John's tail still a wagging.

In the old days before Mr. Volstead, we didn't have to follow a crooked path to a "blind tiger," but stood boldly up with our feet on the brass railing and drank "Old Crow" and "Squirrel Whisky," and in those days most of us had just as leave fly as to climb. We told funny stories and sang foolish songs, and the world was ours—but oh! what a feeling in the morning.

Thirty years ago when I was a young reporter, the boys used to meet in the saloons to while away the time. It was then that I learned that the big men of the city used the saloons for a place to spend their evenings, and the hobo loafed in anticipation of an invitation to take a drink. I also learned that it was here that the politicians met and framed their plans of campaign, and the saloon was our greatest source of information. Enlivened by a few slugs of booze "big men" would give out the information that would often lead to a big story. Then, too, the saloons were the congregating places for all standards and types of men. Here I have seen the judge and the hobo, the politician and the hi-jacker, the church member and the gambler mingling together in blissful ecstacy, where on the streets each would shun the other as they would a skunk in a garlic patch.

We reporters, too, in the old days, found the men who ran the saloons to be our friends—they were notoriously good fellows and performed vastly more generosities than any other class of men. When we simply had to have a few dollars we might go to the office and get it, but there was always quibbling, a reminder of the pay check, and the good advice about cutting down expenses, but who in the devil ever wanted advice when he was trying to borrow money. When some of us boys needed a little cash we went to the saloon keeper and without a word or a question, invariably got the money, without interest and without trouble.

This was the game, the custom and the code. But in the days of our prosperity and on the good old Saturday nights, when the pay envelope was full of coin, we went out of the way, many times several blocks, to spend across the bar of our particular saloon keeper the deferred interest on the loan. And we invariably went reeling to our squalid rooms in the cold gray dawn of the morning, with a bad taste in our mouths and to realize that

"I ain't no hand with the corn juice,
For taking it all along,
You never can till you've drunk it,
And then you are like to be wrong.
There's times when you'll hope you're dying
There's times when you'll wish you were dead;
And the things you'll see after drinking "Alchie"
Will raise the hairs on your head."

I tell you candidly that next to a pretty woman I love a "shot" of whisky best of all, and consequently I frequented the saloons quite a little in the old days. I was standing at the bar in Alva, Okla., with my old friend John Doolin one evening. We were telling each other where all we had been and the sights we had seen. The bar room bum, and there were many of them in Alva at that time, was standing close by hoping to be invited to take a drink. In order to attract our attention, after listening to the wonderful things we had seen, and the wonderful places we had been, he inquired:

"Have either of you fellows ever had delirium tremens?'

"No," I replied, and with a sneer this bar room bum said:

"Hell! You ain't been nowhere and seen nothin'."

Charlie Clovis was a printer I used to work with while in the saloon days at Alva, and Charlie was one "pippin of a scout." We used to stand close by the bar with one foot on the rail and "oil up our running gear" until the small hours of the night. On these occasions life was everything but empty, and our troubles and joys were one grand mixture of delight. On one occasion when we had lingered long Charlie related to me next day how he gravitated home to his dear little wife and by mistake kissed the neighbor's hired man next door. But then he came to himself and slid in home by the back door with a head like a rain barrel, his shoes in his hand, his pants on his arm, only to step on the cat, and then there was the devil to pay.

I wandered into Alva some time ago to look up the fellows I used to run with, and as I hung around the old familiar haunts I couldn't help but wonder, where are the boys with their smiles and their frowns? And my old friend Ike McHenry, who used to dish us out the beer I found serving the boys with iced tea and chili a la mode, and he told me the old gang no longer sailed Green River by a bright morning star, and while their stomachs might be pleading for the olden delight the gang was forced to be content with iced coffee and other such slop.

Fred Fredericks was one of the younger boozers when I was in Alva. Fred liked liquor from every angle. He liked the taste and he liked the effect, and he killed a goodly quantity each and every day. He had a constitution like a mule, and could consume more of the stuff than most of us fellows, but it eventually got his goat. The last time I saw Fred the boys were having a party down on the river, and had been camped out for a week, doing more drinking than anything else. Fred had been stewed to the gills for four or five days. We were walking along the river bank. It was an extremely hot day and a small water snake was laying along the bank in the sun. Fred spied the snake and stopped. He looked at it for several minutes and the little fellow never moved. Not sure of his ground Fred went back to camp and got his gun. Pointing it at the little snake in a husky voice said: "If you are a snake you are in a devil of a fix, if you are not a snake I am in a devil of a fix."

Alva is a 100 per cent American city. Most everybody not born in Alva was born in Medicine Lodge, Kan. There were no foreigners of any character that made that town their home when I lived there, but one day some kind of a Dago looking fellow who was proving up a claim west of the town drifted in and for a week put on a wonderful spree. He was a talkative "cuss" and bored everybody to death. He was a bad man without being dangerous, most of his murders being committed with his mouth. Pearl Maxey became tired of the foreigner's lingo, and organized a few of the boys, consisting chiefly of the rougher element of the little city. The boys wandered around to the different saloons until they found the Dago. Then they began to tank up. With every drink they would invite the Dago to have one, and with every drink and between times the boys would slap and kick and otherwise maltreat the foreigner, but would do it in a jocular way. As the party waxed gay Maxey and one or two of the other boys began to shove the Dago across the room, slap him a little harder, until finally Maxey got in a good lick and knocked him down. When he got up the Dago crawled over behind a lot of whiskey barrels piled up in the back of the saloon and as he slipped down out of sight behind the barrels the fellows heard him say: "Town boys getting drunk all time, all time, all time."

Sefton Knight's wife was the president of the W. C. T. U. in Alva in the good old days, and boasted the fact that Sefton never took a drink in his life. She was the kind of woman that ruled the roost, and when she said walk it Sefton walked it. He was not afraid of her, he would tell the boys, but just somehow or other had a great respect for her. When Jack Ross landed the Science Hall for Alva, which was a big addition to the Northwestern State Normal school, Alva decided to celebrate, and a public barbecue was held in the courthouse yard, at which, among other things, punch was served. One of the boys, whose name I dare not mention, conceived the idea of mixing a large quantity of alcohol with Sefton's glass of punch, and it was done so smoothly that Sefton didn't know about it until the next day. Sefton sipped his punch and talked gloriously of what fine punch it was. Mrs. Sefton thought it the finest punch she ever drank. She sat by the side of her hubby and insisted that he drink more. And when his eyes got the glassy stare and his tongue warbled too freely, she couldn't understand, but when old Sefton began to sing: "All I want is fifty million dollars, with champaign fountains spraying 'round my feet;

Pierpont Morgan waiting on the table, and Sousa's band a playin' while I eat," she became a little suspicious, but she never knew exactly how it happened.

On another occasion I was loafing around the bar in Ike McHenry's saloon at Alva. Someone in the crowd had called for drinks for the house, when the swinging doors flew open and Dixie Dunbar, a tramp printer well known throughout Kansas and Oklahoma in the old days, and who spent more time in the saloons than in the print shops, wandered in, the crowd lined up at the bar with Dixie in the bum's usual place—at the foot. On such occasions men were expected to give a toast before they drank, and none of the formalties were overlooked on this occasion. Each of the men in line had his say. Most of the crowd boasted of their homes, their wives or their children. When the turn came to Dixie Dunbar, the dirty tramp, he held the glass high in his hands as he said:

"I too, once had a home and friends and position. I had a home where love lit the fire on the altar and ministered before it, and I put out the whole fire and darkness and desolation reigned in its stead. I had a wife as beautiful as an artist's dream, and I dropped the priceless pearl of her honor and respect in the wine cup, and, Cleopatra like, saw it dissolve and quaffed it down with the brimming draught. I had children as bright and lovely as the flowers of spring, and I saw them wither and die under the blighting curse of a drunken father. Today I am a husband without a wife, a father without a child, a man with no home to call his own, and all swallowed up in the maelstrom of drink." The glass fell to the counter and was shattered; the swinging doors folded back and Dixie Dunbar slipped out into the darkness.

Later in the night the city marshal called me out of bed and, told me Old Dixie Dunbar was in the city jail suffering the tortures of the damned. I got a doctor and went to relieve him. After the doctor had administered a stiff drink of whiskey and the delirium tremens passed, throughout the night, at intervals, he told me this story:

"As I stood at the bar I saw the delirium coming on and wanted to get away from respectable men. I slipped into the street and all at once and without warning, my reason forsook me. The sidewalks were one masss of living, moving howling ferocious animals. Then a human corpse appeared before me. It had motion, but I knew it was a tenant of that dark and windowless abode, the grave. It opened full upon me its dull, glassy, lustreless eyes; stark, cold and hideous it stood before me. I turned to rush, I knew not where, but my limbs seemed paralyzed. I then thought for a second time that I was dreaming, and awoke and laughed a wild laugh, but I knew I was awake."

There was a gurgling in his throat—the effect of the drink had spent its force, and the spark of life began to fade. For several hours he lingered, fighting the beasts and snakes that did not exist. Next day we laid him to rest in the potter's field, and his tortures were at an end. Shortly afterwards Oklahoma was admitted to the Union, and the saloons passed out of existence, and it only took a few years to convince me that

"Iv'e taken my booze where I've found it,
And now I must pay for my fun,
For the more you drink of this bootleg
The less you will see o' the sun;
And the end o' it's peddling pencils,
Or selling shoe-strings, you see,
So be warned by my lot (which I know you will not)
And learn about liquor from me."

MEMORIES

Some of the Things a Newspaper Reporter Runs Into That Linger With Him Throughout the Remainder of His Life.

"Some time, ol' pard of other days,
I get to ridin' after strays
That drift across ol' Mem'ry's range
To bed where shadows move and change."

Huddled in the corner at the foot of the stairs of The Eagle editorial rooms most any blustery night, may be seen half a dozen "newsies" with their heads pillowed on their arms, sleeping in perfect oblivion to their surroundings. In looking over this aggregation last night, memory carried me back to Jack Maxey, the greatest newsie I ever knew, and I have trailed with a good many of them.

Jack landed in the mailing room of the Louisville Courier-Journal just a few minutes ahead of a blue snow, and according to his announcement, as cool as a cucumber. From all appearances Jack had fought the chilly blasts, not only of the storm, but of an unkind fate, for some ten or twelve winters and was ready to fight the future with the stolid indifference of a locoed steer in fly time. Of his home, his parents and his past he was as silent as a speckled trout in a dead eddy, but from other sources it was learned that he was left an orphan a year previous, and had spent most of that time dodging through alleys, eating slumgullion from garbage cans, and fighting for an existence with about the same degree of success as a Digger Indian gulping down a gourd of grasshopper soup.

Will Harbison had charge of the "newsies" and was dishing out papers when Jack wanted in, and the glitter of fire in Jack's eye seemed to touch his withered old heart, and he staked the kid to a bundle of papers and started him on the streets as a full-fledged newsboy.

Since Mother Eve produced Cain and Abel and they followed in the footsteps of their parents and started a crop of boys of their own, it has been the custom to try out the grit, staying qualities and nerve of every new kid who enters the newsie gang, and before the day was over Jack had been weighed in the balance and found not wanting. The bigger boys taunted him, laughed at his shabby clothes, made fun of his red hair, but failed to arouse his smouldering ire until Ned Evans made a slighting remark about his parentage. The remark brought the fire to Jack's eyes, set him to breathing hard, and he flew into Ned like a speckled guinea at a bulldog.

When the dust cleared away Ned's general appearance was likened unto a cotton-tailed rabbit that had been run through a threshing machine. He was bleeding from bites, kicks, scratches and bruises from the knot that kept his backbone from raveling out to the "gluts" that pushed him along the street. He had run into a tiger while looking for a mouse, and Jack Maxey had been initiated as a member of the newsie gang—the pride of half a dozen boys who had not fared so well at the hands of Ned Evans.

Barney Corrigan was a wealthy cattle man down in Oklahoma when I first moved to Alva. He made thousands of dollars out of cattle and in his old age is a pauper—his fortune gone and his manhood sold at cost. He ran big herds on the rich buffalo grass of western Woods county and became rich. Then he became enamored with a "gold digger," and today he is poor, indeed. It was the story of the old king, who in his drunkenness laughed at her antics, and I can hear the echo of that laugh resounding down the ages. I knew Corrigan and his wife for 15 years before the crash came, and he lived happily with his little family during that time. After he made his fortune it went to his head and he moved to town, and got caught in the web.

As age crept on, the good wife devoted more of her time to the children. The shows were given up, card parties were not planned, motherly duty demanded her time, and it was at this period in life when Barney met the gold digger. Barney didn't know it then, and his friends couldn't tell him, that she was a beautiful woman beckoning to a weak man, leading him over the hill to the cemetery. But in later years he realized how wise the old monks were in going to monasteries where they could get away from woman's clutches. In the past year I have heard him say that the "thinking man on life's highway is wont to pause when faced by the perils of a crisis caused by the trivial attitude of womankind which bids fair to destroy his very being, and ask himself the meaning of the senseless struggle for existence. And Barney paid the price. Today he is an old man, sitting on a tombstone, thinking. He can get no consolation from the old story of Eden over again, by whimpering that the woman tempted him.

Barney Corrigan lost his cattle ranch and every dollar he had in the world, and the gold digger got most of it, only to let it get away. Today Barney is beating back at $25 a week, paying his last year's bills, and the men around the stock yards who knew him of old, know him now as only a memory or a bad dream.

More than 25 centuries have passed since Jeremiah on a hillside in Judea uttered this searching phrase: "O, foolish people that have eyes and see not," and there has been but little change in the general make-up of a weak man filtered down through the ages.

Bill Apperson and Rowland Dallas were known as the smoothest guys in the little Kentucky town in which I was raised. The crimes laid at their doors were many, but their smooth workings always let them out.

They thought of many days of luxurious idleness as they fixed the fuse to a shot of nitro glycerine in the vault door of the safe in the Nelson Brothers general store, one of the largest mercantile establishments in the city, wherein, minus a bank in the little town, the citizens kept their savings. But overlooking a small detail caused the smoothest of guys to come to grief, and although it was 20 or more years ago these men are still paying the debt they owe to the county and state, which already has taken most of their lives. Clever, well organized, experienced, they overlooked one little thing for which they are still paying. And they have realized that the old prophet knew what he was talking about when he said "be sure your sins will find you out." And the same holds good today equally as well as it did so many years ago.

These experts were prepared for possible interruptions. Wires were cut before the work started, and the lookouts were active gunmen. Citizens next door to the building were awakened by the rumble and arose, attempting to turn on the lights. The light was as hurriedly extinguished when a shot whizzed through the window and Charley Bledsoe was killed.

A handcar stolen from a work gang on the railroad waited on the tracks for the men when the job was done. The door blew out. The margin of safety was drawing to a close. In haste they grabbed a sack of coin. Thousands of dollars in bills overlooked in the mess within the vault, they dashed from the building. The lookout scouts scattered. They headed for the tracks and the waiting handcar. Then came one oversight in their nearly perfect plan.

They had cut the wires leading to the central telephone office. But in the tangled mass that came as they snipped, they overlooked the one line over which warning could pass direct to the town marshal's office. It was the direct cable, and as they fled it carried the message and the warning over the country to watch the tracks.

The two men were down the tracks far ahead of their pursuers, but as they approached a nearby town they were greeted with a volley of shots. Farmers along the line had received the word and hastened to the railroad tracks. They fired in the dark, across a long bridge. The bandits jumped and the handcar disappeared. Posses searched during the day. Finally inspecting a haystack, carelessly jabbing the sides, a bald head popped out and a bandit was in custody. In the stack the other man was soon located.

Twenty years ago Bill Apperson and Rowland Dallas began serving a life sentence in the penitentiary. Twenty-five years ago they were boys in a little Kentucky town, as care free, and wild as the boys of today, little knowing or caring about the prophecy of the old king who wrote many years ago: "Be sure your sins will find you out."

Minnie Copass was the belle of her set in the little Oklahoma town in which I lived a dozen or more years ago. Of poor but respectable parents, she grew to girlhood a beautiful and refined young lady.

Bob Snavely, too, was born of respectable parents, but proved the age-old story that has wafted down the pages of time, that "a good mother sometimes bears a bad son."

In the summer when the gardens were aglow with blue and red, Minnie fell in love with Bob and they ran away and were married. It was against the will of her parents, but when they found it out it was too late, for a staid old minister had tied the knot with the solemn provision that "what God has joined together let no man put asunder."

Sped the months and came the sheriff, and Charley was sent to the penitentiary on a charge of highway robbery.

Down at Oklahoma City there are three men known as the parole board, who meet every so often and listen to pleas of relatives and friends for the parole of criminals. The board was hearing the requests for paroles. Minnie told her story and plead with tears in her eyes and a wee little baby in her arms, for the release of her husband.

"Call the little girl back," said the chairman of the board. An officer opened the door to the private chamber and beckoned the young mother to enter. They called back her wayward husband, and in her presence and his, read to her the confession he had made—a confession admitting the crime and also admitting that he had lived with another girl while married to her; that he had been untrue to his marriage vows and to the laws of his state and his country. And when she objected to the other girl he had struck the young wife; that a policeman saw him strike her and made the arrest, and then he admitted his other crimes. "Now, were we to parole him, would you live with him?" they asked.

The little wife and mother nodded her head emphatically. "You have fallen for him pretty hard, haven't you?" queried a member of the board.

"I certainly have," was the girl's response, as she brushed aside the boy's crime and his infidelity. "I love him," was her defense, her explanation for all her avowals of faith in her faithless husband.

The board listened, but with stony hearts, and the chairman said: "Take him back to a cell, he is not fit to live at large in any community."

The young wife and mother cried, softly and silently. She wanted her husband. She wanted to give him another chance.

The prison board rustled the papers on their desk. It was the signal to clear the room. The little wife, wild eyed, tried to be brave. The boy hung his head. The huge bar door that shut him away from his wife and child clanged with a harsh, grating sound.

Then methought, that love can save a bad man as well as ruin a good one, as be like the peace of God himself, past all understanding. And I wondered if that Oklahoma parole board had made a mistake.

√